Thorsons
Calorie Counter

Thorsons
Calorie Counter

Thorsons
An Imprint of HarperCollins*Publishers*

Thorsons
An Imprint of HarperCollins*Publishers*
77—85 Fulham Palace Road,
Hammersmith, London W6 8JB

Published by Thorsons 1995

10 9 8 7 6 5 4 3 2

© Virtual City Associates 1995

A catalogue record for this book
is available from the British Library

ISBN 0 7225 3190 7

Typeset by Harper Phototypesetters Limited,
Northampton, England
Printed in Great Britain by
HarperCollinsManufacturing Glasgow

Contents

Medical Warning

This book is for the basically healthy adult who wishes to lose (or gain) modest amounts of weight. Every calorie-controlled diet should also contain a well-balanced range of essential nutrients. People who have, or have relatives with, diabetes, high blood-pressure, heart disease or allergies of any kind, or who have suffered from any other serious disease, should seek medical advice before trying any form of dieting. There are also a number of illnesses that can result in weight gain or weight loss, which a diet alone will not address. Children, pregnant women and those in athletic programmes should also only diet on medical advice. The text in this book should be read in its entirety. In fact, if you have the slightest doubt, consult a doctor or qualified nutritionist.

Acknowledgements

The nutritional material in this book has come from a variety of manufacturers, supermarkets, on-line information databases, and UK and US official sources. All brand names are hereby acknowledged. Particular help was received from Allied Bakeries Limited, Asda Stores Ltd, Baxters of Speyside Limited, Birds Eye Wall's Limited, Boots The Chemists Ltd, Brooke Bond Foods Ltd, Budgens Stores Limited, C Shippam Limited, Cadbury Ltd, Campbell Grocery Products Limited, Co-op Wholesale Society, Dairy Crest Limited, H J Heinz Company Ltd, Holland and Barrett, J A Sharwood & Co Ltd, John West Foods Limited, Kellogg Company of Great Britain Ltd, Kraft General Foods Ltd, Marks and Spencer plc, Nestlé UK Ltd, Northumbrian Fine Foods plc, Reckitt & Colman Products Limited, Safeway Stores plc, Sainsbury's plc, Sovereign Chicken Limited, St Ivel, The Jacob's Bakery Limited, The New Covent Garden Soup Co Ltd, UB (Ross Young's) Ltd, United Biscuits (UK) Limited, W Jordan (Cereals) Ltd, Waitrose Limited, and Whole Earth Foods Ltd. The UK official source was McCance and Widdowson: *The Composition of Foods* (Fifth Edition), used by permission of the Royal Society of Chemistry and the Comptroller of Her Majesty's Stationery Office. We'd like to acknowledge the editorial assistance of Sam Edwards.

How to Use This Book

- Read the primer on calorie counting, diet and nutrition beginning on page 11.

- Weigh yourself and compare your weight with the figures in the tables beginning on page 18.

- Take a look at your lifestyle and eating patterns, using the information on pages 20–26, and calculate the amount of energy you use up during your average day from the figures in the tables beginning on page 21.

- Analyse your existing diet and estimate your daily energy intake from the foods you eat from the figures in the tables beginning on page 34.

- Set a realistic target for weight loss (or weight gain).

- Design or adapt a diet that will meet that target, using your analysis of your lifestyle and eating patterns and the calorie values in the schemes beginning on page 29.

Introduction

Why is it so important to have an up-to-date calorie counter? Because the foods we buy from shops and supermarkets keep on changing. In 1991 there were over 2800 grocery product launches in the UK alone; probably almost as many products vanished from the shelves. But this figure understates the extent of the changes; it doesn't include product variants — new flavours, new recipe formulations. Even less visibly, pack sizes may be adjusted, or recipes subtly altered to reflect market conditions, or the changing prices of raw commodities. Nor does the figure fully include the 'own' or 'private' brands of the big supermarkets, and buying groups are almost certainly under-represented. One recent survey says private labels in supermarkets account for 54 per cent of all sales.

Every time a pack is altered the calorific value changes. Judging from our own research for this edition of *Thorsons Calorie Counter*, the areas that show the greatest change are ready-made foods, frozen foods, dairy products, bakery and confectionery. We have had to rewrite completely both the ready-made and sandwich sections.

Over a period of time, even the calorific value of basics such as fresh meat cuts may change — usually because cattle and pigs are reared to be less fatty and because we the public have asked our butchers to trim off more fat.

So — a calorie counter that is more than two or so years old is almost useless.

Calorie Counting

According to a Gallup opinion poll in 1992, at least 20 per cent of the UK population is at any one time trying to slim; 59 per cent of men and 60 per cent of women think they are overweight.

The idea of calorie counting flows in and out of fashion. Any number of diet books offer allegedly simple rules for weight control: lists of 'good' and 'bad' foods, collections of recipes, miracle ingredients, and so on. But if they work at all, at the back of all of them someone somewhere is counting calories.

The drawback of so many of these schemes is their lack of flexibility; the advantage of a guide to calories is that you possess the basic information from which to adapt an existing plan or formulate your own.

Flexibility is more important now than ever because the life-styles most of us lead today are very different from those described in most diet books. They nearly all make an assumption: that our eating habits are centred on 'three square meals a day'. Implicitly all the advice given concentrates on changing the food we eat during those three meals to reduce their calorific content. The fact is, beginning in the 1980s and accelerating fast in the 1990s, many of us don't eat in that way at all – we 'snack' and we 'munch', that is, we are abandoning many formal meals and simply eat when we feel hungry.

Sales of chilled foods, the basis of so much convenience eating, grew by almost 12 per cent each year between 1988 and 1992. In fact, our national diet is changing more rapidly than you may realize. All of us are buying less basic or generic food in favour of convenience products. Compared with 10 years ago we are buying 16 per cent less unprocessed meat. Sales of fresh and frozen fish fell by 13 per cent between 1991 and 1992 – in favour of cooked varieties. We are also buying fewer fresh vegetables, other than those that can be eaten immediately, a fall of over 20 per cent during the aforementioned decade. Frozen vegetables, however, increased their sales by 7 per cent in 1992; and sales of frozen ready meals leapt by 17 per cent. Only three per cent of us were vegetarians in 1986; that had doubled to 6 per cent by 1991 and 10 per cent of the population may have abandoned meat by the end of the decade.

Any diet plan which ignores these important social changes is probably not going to work.

Our changed lifestyles mean that both sides of the 'calorie-controlled diet' equation — our energy needs as a result of *how we spend our day* and our energy intake in the form of *what we eat* — have undergone profound alterations. Here, in a pocketable form, you'll be able to make your plans — and continue to live with them.

> **Although people who diet normally wish to reduce their weight, some people need to gain weight — this book is for you as well.**

Our Changing Lifestyles

Let's look at the social changes that were mentioned a little more closely; you may be able to recognize yourself in them. Many people still think that the 'normal' living arrangement consists of a family made up of a male adult, a female adult and one to two children. In fact, only one quarter of all UK households fall into this pattern. There are actually more households made up of just one person. Another 27 per cent are married couples with no children.

Now, if you live by yourself, conventional meals can

sometimes be a bit of a bother — you may skip some in exchange for several snacks or take-aways. If you have no children you may feel less pressure always to eat at the same time, or mostly at the same place.

Work patterns also dictate our eating habits. By 1988, women made up 48 per cent of the work-force. We know the reasons well enough: a mixture of greater emancipation and a desire for a proper career — and an economic need to support the family. But a working woman approaches meals and meal preparation very differently from one whose main role is to look after the house and family. Again: many of us, men and women, are expected by our employers to work shifts. Nearly half of those employed work at weekends, 12 per cent do shift work based on the ordinary working day, and just under 2 per cent work nights. All of this has an enormous effect on *when* we eat as well as *what* we eat. This affects not only those who actually do the shift work, but everyone who lives with them, including children. Working in shifts means eating in shifts. There is a hidden hazard here, for slimmers: you may tend to eat with your loved ones as well as when you yourself are hungry — simply as a way of sharing some time with them.

There has been one other change during the last decade: many of us are having to travel longer distances to work. Some of us have voluntarily abandoned the inner suburbs in order to live in a healthier and cleaner environment; others have found that a house or flat big enough for their needs is just too expensive in the city. Longer commutes means abandoned breakfasts, sneaked snacks in the morning, later evening meals and, to compensate, more sneaked snacks in the late afternoon. The energy content of many favourite snacks can cause severe disruption to any diet plan.

This changed lifestyle also affects our patterns of hunger and appetite — we may feel hungry at times of the day when it is inconvenient to prepare and eat 'healthy' food. Our stomachs crave satisfaction when all that is available is instant junk food. Unless we are very aware of what is going on, any controlled diet scheme will soon fall to pieces. What is worse, many of us are sufficiently weak-willed to tell ourselves that such snacks don't really count: 'It doesn't matter that I had a quick packet of crisps or a biscuit, because my main meal of the day came with a "Low Calorie" label on it.' Check out the calorie tables for crisps and biscuits in this book, and see if you can still kid yourself!

The food industry — both manufacturers and retailers — have risen to the challenge of our new lifestyles. Chill-cooked (or half-cooked) foods, new packaging methods, and new semi-instant foods to be cooked rapidly in microwaves have all become occasional parts (and sometimes staples) of our diet. The food and supermarket industries refer to these as 'recipe dishes', but the term 'ready-made meals' has been used in this book.

The traditional formal meal hasn't completely disappeared, of course, and it still plays an important role in all our lives — but look carefully at the last week or two of your life: how much of your diet was made up of informal snacking and munching?

Calorie Counting: A Quick Primer

This is not meant to be a full-blown guide to nutrition, but some explanations are essential if this book is to help you.

A calorie is a measure of the energy content of food. All foods have a calorific value and contribute to keeping the body going. A high calorific value means that there is a lot of energy locked up in the food which the body can convert. The various demands we make of our bodies — breathing, walking, talking, running, lifting and so on — all require energy, and this too can be measured in calories.

(Strictly speaking, the scientific unit of energy is the Joule.

If you look at the nutritional tables on most food packages you will find that energy values are expressed both in calories and in Joules. One calorie is the amount of heat required to raise the temperature of 1 gram of water by 1 degree centigrade. Since that is a very small amount of heat, the convenient unit for nutritional calculations is actually the kilocalorie, 1000 calories, abbreviated to kcal. So what we call calories are in fact kilocalories. The Joule is also too small for convenient use and nutritionists operate in kiloJoule units (kJ). The conversion factor is: 1 kilocalorie equals 4.184 kJ.)

The principles of the calorie-controlled diet are perfectly simple: using the set of tables beginning on page 21 you first take a look at your daily activities and calculate your individual energy requirement. Using the main Calorie Counter tables (beginning on page 34) you identify the energy content of the food you eat. In ideal circumstances the two figures should be identical. If you take in more food energy than your body burns up, some of it will be evacuated when you use the toilet, but some will stay in your body, typically deposited as fat, and your weight will increase. If you don't eat enough of the right sort of energy-giving food, then your body will have to draw on its own resources and use up existing stores of fat. Essentially, that's what you make your body do when you go on a traditional slimming diet.

Like many simple explanations, some important details are overlooked here, however.

First, there is of course more to food than its energy content. We require substantial amounts of water, both as a liquid and 'trapped' or integrated into solid foods. Besides water, we require a wide range of vitamins and minerals. We also need a collection of proteins, and although proteins are one of the main sources of energy, quite apart from this they are essential to life. We must also have fibre (strictly speaking, fibre isn't a food because it is not ingested, however the alimentary canal requires it in order to function properly and ingest the 'true' foods).

So: you can't base a diet solely on calorie counting. Indeed, one of the many dangers of crash weight-loss courses is that the body ends up lacking essential nutrients. Whatever your plans, you must have what nutritionists call a 'well-balanced diet'. In general terms, this means eating a broad range of fresh foods, with an emphasis on uncooked (or only slightly cooked) fruit and vegetables. These foods should bring you all the proteins, vitamins and minerals your body needs.

Second, the way in which the body actually handles food is rather more complicated than the simple 'energy in/energy out' explanation.

The energy-supplying ingredients in food are: proteins, carbohydrates, fats and alcohol. Alcohol isn't normally thought of as a food because of its other, well-known effects, but it does supply energy.

Protein
Protein is made up of amino acids. There are 20 key amino acids. Eight of these are called essential amino acids because their nutrients cannot be manufactured by the body and must come from the outside, from our diet. Excess protein taken in is burned for energy. One gram of protein burned for its energy contains four calories.

Carbohydrate
Carbohydrates are the body's main source of energy. Other energy nutrients must be converted to carbohydrate before the body can use them. Carbohydrates provide glucose ready for the body to burn. But the body can also convert fat and protein to glucose, and will do so if the need arises. This is why starvation causes muscle tissue to waste away: living

muscle proteins are burned for their energy. This takes place after the main fat stores in the body have been exhausted.

Carbohydrates can be classed as simple or complex. A simple carbohydrate is a mono- or di-saccharide. Examples of simple carbohydrates are glucose, fructose (found in fruit), sucrose and lactose (found in milk). Complex carbohydrates are polysaccharides, long chains of glucose molecules, more commonly referred to as starch. These take much longer to digest, because the body has to take them apart, one molecule at a time. One gram of carbohydrate contains four calories of energy, and people require a minimum of about 100 grams a day.

Fats
Fats are a concentrated energy source, yielding nine calories per gram, compared to the four per gram found in protein and carbohydrate. Nutritionally, fats exist in three different chemical states: saturated, monounsaturated and poly-unsaturated. Generally, the more unsaturated a given fatty acid, the more liquid the fat is. Saturated fats are associated with heart disease because fatty deposits can build up in the body's blood vessels and slow down blood flow; poly-unsaturates, being more liquid, are less likely to do this — hence the health claims.

We refer to 'fats' as those that are solid at room temperature, and 'oils' as those that are liquid. Fat that comes from animals is almost always a 'fat'; that which come from plants is almost always an 'oil'. This is because plants construct unsaturated fats, while animals can only synthesize saturated fats. Animals can only get energy by eating it, and so need a concentrated storage medium. Fat is that medium. Excess energy is converted to fat and stored until it is needed. The human body is especially efficient at this task.

Alcohol

Alcohol is also a nutrient, in that it provides energy and contains calories. One gram of pure alcohol produces about 7 calories, which the body can and does utilize as an energy source. The alcohol in 100 ml of 70-proof whisky has about 200 calories. Alcohol is not a fat, nor a carbohydrate, nor a protein, but behaves like a fat in some respects and like a carbohydrate in others.

Food Combining

A good diet should probably take about one third (37 per cent) of its calories from (mostly complex, or starchy) carbohydrates, one third (30 per cent) from protein, and one third (33 per cent) from fat (mostly polyunsaturated).

In practice, this 37/30/33 ratio is far from perfect. The basic idea, if you're trying to lose weight, is to reduce the amount of fat you take in, replacing its calories with other sources of energy. Fat, *per se*, has few vitamins and minerals, though vitamins A and D are important exceptions. Fat is chiefly only calories.

You also need to pay attention to the different sources of carbohydrate. Sugars provide the quickest source of energy, which is why glucose tablets and drinks are so useful when you feel exhausted, but many sugary snacks are also 'empty carbohydrates' in that they *only* provide energy and none of the other essential nutrients. A slimmer should always seek foods that deliver additional nutritional benefits besides pure energy. If you eat too many snacks to satisfy an immediate hunger, the excess may get converted into fat. Starch gets converted into energy more slowly, and a few starchy foods — bread, pasta, root vegetables, beans, cereals — also contain other important nutrients and fibre.

Fat Conversion

Not all bodies are equally good at converting excess energy into fat. Let's put it another way — some people are prone to fatness and some are not. Two people can eat identically sized meals; one will evacuate all that is not required and one will store the excess as fat — around the stomach if he is a man, around the hips and thighs if she is a woman. There is no real 'explanation' for this. And there aren't just these two types of people, there is a progressive scale between those who are essentially 'thinnies' and those who are 'fatties'. It is the 'fatties', of course, who have to be more concerned with calorie control. They have got one clear advantage over 'thinnies', though: a thin person who suffers from a long illness will usually take longer to achieve full recovery than a fat one, because there are less fat reserves to draw upon.

There is one other feature about how fat is stored in the body that is critical to understanding the problems of weight control. A fat cell in the body is composed of one part of fat to 4 to 5 parts water. This explains why 'it is so hard to take off, so easy to put on': 10 grams of solid 'energy food' taken in and then stored as fat may show up as 50 or 60 grams of added body weight. It also explains why the first week of a diet always seems to produce extremely good results — you are losing the trapped water.

What You Should Weigh

These are average tables, with figures in pounds and kilograms. Although you may be more used to thinking in terms of pounds, you'll find calculations are easier if you switch to kilograms.

The figures have been derived from tables produced by life assurance companies; allowance has been made for the fact that some of us have bigger frames, broader shoulders, stockier builds and heavier bones than others. Be honest with yourself, though, and try and visualize what you'd like your body to look like. There is also an instant 'skin-fold' test you can try to see if you are carrying excess weight: stand naked in front of a mirror and see how big a fold of flesh you can pinch out from your tummy area or your buttocks or thighs. If the fold is more than 3 cm (just over an inch) without causing any tautening of surrounding flesh — you are carrying extra weight.

How to Weigh Yourself

- Always use the same scales.
- Weigh yourself at the same time of day. Most people wait until their stomach is empty, but whatever you do keep to one pattern. Your lowest weight of the day is usually first thing in the morning.
- Wear more or less the same clothes each time. (The tables assume you are wearing 2 to 3 kilograms — 5 to 6 lb of clothing).
- Use the scales properly. Make sure they are firmly set on an even floor and read zero when no one is standing on them. Stand with your weight evenly distributed.

Men: desirable weights in outdoor clothing

Height Ft in/cm	Small Frame lb/kg		Medium Frame lb/kg		Large Frame lb/kg	
5'2 158	112-120	50.5-54.5	118-129	53.5-58.5	126-141	57.0-64.0
5'3 160	115-123	52.0-56.0	121-133	55.0-60.5	129-144	58.5-65.0
5'4 163	118-128	53.5-57.0	124-136	56.0-62.0	132-148	60.0-67.0
5'5 165	121-129	55.0-58.5	127-139	57.5-63.0	135-152	61.0-67.0
5'6 168	124-133	56.0-60.5	130-143	58.5-65.0	138-156	62.5-71.0
5'7 170	128-137	58.0-62.0	134-147	61.0-66.5	142-161	64.5-73.0
5'8 173	132-141	60.0-64.0	138-152	64.5-71.0	147-166	66.5-75.5
5'9 175	136-145	62.0-66.0	142-156	64.5-71.0	151-170	68.5-77.0
5'10 178	140-150	63.5-68.0	146-160	66.0-72.5	155-174	70.0-79.0
5'11 180	144-154	65.0-70.0	150-165	68.0-75.0	159-179	72.0-81.0
6'0 183	148-158	67.0-71.5	154-170	70.0-77.0	164-184	74.5-83.5
6'1 185	152-162	69.0-73.5	158-175	71.5-79.0	168-189	76.0-85.5
6'2 188	156-167	71.0-76.0	162-180	73.5-81.5	173-194	78.5-88.0
6'3 190	160-171	72.5-77.5	167-185	76.0-84.0	178-199	80.5-90.5
6'4 193	164-175	74.5-79.0	172-190	78.0-86.0	182-204	82.5-92.5

Women: desirable weights in outdoor clothing

Height Ft in/cm	Small Frame lb/kg		Medium Frame lb/kg		Large Frame lb/kg	
4'10 147	92-98	41.5-44.5	96-107	43.5-48.5	104-119	47.0-54.0
4'11 149	94-101	42.5-46.0	98-110	44.5-50.0	106-122	48.0-55.0
5'0 152	96-104	43.5-47.0	101-113	46.0-51.0	109-125	49.5-56.5
5'1 155	99-107	45.0-48.5	104-116	47.0-52.5	112-128	51.0-58.0
5'2 158	102-110	46.5-50.0	107-119	48.5-54.0	115-131	52.0-59.5
5'3 160	105-113	47.5-51.0	110-122	50.0-55.5	118-134	53.5-61.0
5'4 163	108-116	49.0-52.5	113-126	51.0-57.0	121-138	55.0-62.5
5'5 165	112-120	50.5-54.5	118-130	53.5-58.5	126-141	57.0-64.0
5'6 168	115-123	52.0-56.0	121-133	55.0-60.5	129-144	58.5-65.0
5'7 170	118-128	53.5-57.0	124-136	56.0-62.0	132-148	60.0-67.0
5'8 173	121-129	55.0-58.5	127-139	57.5-63.0	135-152	61.0-67.0
5'9 175	124-133	56.0-60.5	130-143	58.5-65.0	138-156	62.5-71.0
5'10 178	128-137	58.0-62.0	134-147	61.0-66.5	142-161	64.5-73.0
5'11 180	132-141	60.0-64.0	138-152	64.5-71.0	147-166	66.5-75.5
6'0 183	136-145	62.0-66.0	142-156	64.5-71.0	151-170	68.5-77.0

Stones and Pounds

Stones	lb	Stones	lb
6.5	91	13.5	189
7.0	98	14.0	196
7.5	105	14.5	203
8.0	112	15.0	210
8.5	119	15.5	217
9.0	126	16.0	224
9.5	133	16.5	231
10.0	140	17.0	238
10.5	147	17.5	245
11.0	154	18.0	252
11.5	161	18.5	259
12.0	168	19.0	266
12.5	175	19.5	273
13.0	182	20.0	280

Taking a Look at Your Lifestyle

Before you can set yourself dietary targets you need to
analyse a few things: In the first place, you need to know how
much energy you use up during the day.

How Much Energy Does Your Body Use?

Using tables, nutritionists can work out fairly accurately the
precise amount of energy you need to function during your
normal day.

First, so much is needed simply to keep your body alive,
even if you are doing no more than lying in bed staring at
the ceiling. This figure is called either your *Resting Energy*

Requirement or your *Basal Metabolic Rate*. The table below shows the resting energy requirement for various people. Here are some averages:

	Weight (kg)	kcal /hr	kcal /day
Infant, 1 year old	10	21	500
Child, 8 years old	25	42	1000
Adult female	55	54	1300
Adult male	65	67	1600

Now, a more accurate figure, based on any weight — multiply this figure by your weight in kilograms:

	kcal /kg/hr	kcal /kg/day
Infant	2.1	50
Child	1.6	40
Adult — male and female	1.0	24

Second, here are figures for the average amount of energy one would use during various sorts of activity during the day. They are based on someone weighing 65 kg. If you weigh a little more you could expect to use a little more energy, if you weigh under 65 kg your body would need a little less. The figures in the left-hand column are expressed in calories-per-hour, the right-hand column gives the rate for 10 minutes of an activity.

Activity	Cal/hr	Cal/10 min
Aerobics, average	430	72
Circuit-training	510	85
Climbing stairs	660	110
Cycling, racing	660	110
Cycling, relaxed	240	40
Cycling, uphill	600	100
Dancing, fast	410	68
Dancing, relaxed	380	63
Driving a car	120	20
Gardening, digging	480	80
Gardening, weeding	210	35
Golf	390	65
Hill-climbing	480	80
Hill-climbing with a back-pack	510	85
Horse-riding, moderate	100	17
Horse-riding, trot	300	50
House-cleaning	240	40
Knitting	90	15
Playing piano	150	25
Running, fast	400	67
Running, slow	280	47
Running, medium jogging	330	55
Shopping	240	40
Sitting	90	15
Skiing	390	65
Sleeping	60	10
Squash	840	140

Activity	Cal/hr	Cal/10 min
Swimming, fast	600	100
Swimming, relaxed	510	85
Tennis	420	70
Typing	120	20
Walking, normal	240	40
Walking quickly	360	60
Weight training	420	70
Work, heavy manual	450	75
Work, light industrial	240	40
Work, moderately heavy	400	67
Writing	120	20

Once you have some idea of how much energy you burn in a given day, you must next add up the calorific value of the food you normally eat during the course of your day. But there is a third factor: you also need to know *when* you eat.

When Do You Eat?
In these days of snacks and 'eating-on-demand' it is important to keep track of your eating habits. You need to be aware of your patterns of *hunger* and *appetite*. Hunger is when your body demands to be fed, appetite is about your taste preferences.

Our changed lifestyle patterns mean that the times we feel hungry may be quite unexpected. If we find ourselves eating both when our bodies send us pangs of hunger and on those occasions when social conventions expect us to — traditional meal times, in other words — our calorie intake is likely to go up dramatically. In addition, if we haven't identified the times of the day when we are likely to feel hungry, we have almost no chance of developing a properly disciplined calorie-controlled diet.

Here are some examples of the new 'snacking' lifestyles and the implications for calorie intake. The examples shown here are for people who are not on any sort of diet:

	kcal
Stay-at-home mother, one pre-school child, one child in education, partner with 'regular' job	
early morning tea	70
breakfast	680
snack after returning from taking older child to school	110
elevenses during shopping	410
munching during lunch preparation	80
lunch	470
snack while feeding younger child	110
snack with older child on its return from school	110
munching during evening meal preparation	90
evening meal with partner	790
late night snack	120
	2940
Executive who travels a great deal	
early morning coffee	70
on-road breakfast	870
coffee and biscuits during first visit	190
coffee and biscuits during second visit	230
lunch	1130

	kcal
tea and biscuits during third visit	190
snack during petrol fill-up	460
tea during fourth visit	70
early evening drink and snack	420
evening meal	1070
late evening snack	120
	4820

Factory worker on afternoon shift

early morning tea and toast	310
late breakfast	680
elevenses	230
lunch	1020
arrival at work snack	90
late afternoon snack	130
arrival at home snack	120
evening meal	980
late evening snack	120
	3680

If you think these calculations are exaggerated, think again: for the most part the size of the main meals has been adjusted downwards to allow for the increase in the number of snacks.

Your body, like any other machine, should be fuelled shortly before it is expected to work. For this reason it is far better to eat a good, nourishing and energy-giving breakfast, give it a few minutes to digest, and let that take you through the morning. If you are on a slimming diet, you will find there is far less temptation to have mid-morning snacks. Almost certainly the foods that make up breakfast (cereal, orange juice, tea or coffee) are far more nourishing overall and far less full of calories weight-for-weight than the sugary and starchy materials that makes up so many small snacks. If at all possible, your lunch and evening meals should be about the same size. The lunch should keep you going throughout the afternoon and the evening meal should be designed to do no more than prevent hunger pains from keeping you awake at night. If you concentrate most of your day's eating into the evening, too much of the food energy will get absorbed into your body while you sleep and, instead of being put to work immediately, it will start the chemical process which converts it into deposits of fat.

The best pattern of all, from the standpoint of your metabolism, is frequent (low-calorie) 'snacking' — but no main meals. Each snack should be around 200 calories, and afterwards there should be an opportunity for proper digestion — no eating on the run. But the snacks have to provide a balanced and complete diet, and that might not be particularly easy.

There is another reason for examining your eating habits. If you are too fat, you will almost certainly find that you have developed a strong preference for foods that will carry on making you fat. You must change your tastes, if only gradually. You must wean your taste buds off the high-calorie foods they may at present prefer.

The Calorie Tables

The calorie listings in this book attempt to use a scheme which is practical for the reader rather than going all out for 'scientific' consistency.

Most food is — still — basically a natural product. For this reason the actual energy and nutritional value of a given dish may vary from what the tables suggest. The amount of sugar in fruit increases as it ripens; the amount of fat in meat increases as the animal grows older. Recipes for the same dish may vary slightly. Even for such standard items as regular pasteurized milk an examination of the cartons sold by the UK's leading supermarkets will show that the energy content varies slightly. So: treat all the values given here as almost, rather than completely, accurate.

Within each category a representative range has been selected – clearly it was impossible to include every food, every way to cook a food and every brand-name product. This would make for a great deal of pointless repetition. In a typical large UK supermarket you could expect to find up to 3000 'own brand' food items. For each of these there will be at least three or four competitors from named producers, but in some cases there may be twenty. And there are, depending on how you count them up, nine or ten major UK supermarket chains.

In the tables you should find all the basic foods and ingredients plus a wide range of less popular 'generic' foods. A 'generic' ingredient or dish is one not sold by brand name. 'Wholemeal bread' is a generic name; 'Hovis' is a brand. The listings include a wide range of branded products but concentrate on the brand-leaders and others that are somehow typical.

For convenience, the tables have been arranged into a series of broad categories – bread, fruit, fish, meat, and so on. However, with the increase in the range of 'just heat it up' food products, it is becoming increasingly difficult to decide where to place them – is the best home for a supermarket's own-brand version of chill-cooked lasagne pescatori in Pasta, Fish or Recipe Dishes, for example? Again, similar foods appear in a variety of packs and 'finishes' – fresh, frozen, chilled, canned – and these days they can be displayed almost anywhere in a supermarket. Judging by the organization of the dietary information material sent to us by the leading UK supermarkets, they have no definitive answers either. This means you may have to look in more than one place in the book to find the food in which you are immediately interested. However, both cross-referencing and an index are provided (page 261).

The inclusion of one branded product rather than another or one from a particular supermarket 'own-brand' range doesn't imply some hidden quality test. The aim has been to provide a sufficient range so that you can guess at the calorific values of almost anything you are likely to come across. Occasionally different brands are included to make a point – either that apparently dissimilar items have the same calorific value, or that dishes sold under almost identical names may have been made from quite a wide variety of recipes and hence display a surprising range of energy contents.

Generic items are usually quoted in kilocalories per 100 grams (kcal/100 g), making it easy to compare different sorts of food. 100 grams is about 3.5 imperial ounces. Fluids are quoted in kcal/100 ml (millilitres) – that is one tenth of a litre, 3.5 fluid ounces or 0.175 of an imperial pint. (A US pint is 16 fluid ounces compared to the imperial's 20 fluid ounces. 1 millilitre, is the same as 1 cubic centimetre, cc.) Where it helps there may also be calculations for individual portions, but people's views vary on what constitutes a reasonable-sized portion.

Bear in mind that many foods contain inedible elements such as bone, skin or pips. You should compare our suggestions with what you actually put on a plate. Remember also that some items may need reconstituting with water before you eat them and this will drastically change the calorific value per 100 grams. In fact, any form of cooking will change the calorific value per 100 grams, either by adding water or, as in the case of toasting, by removing it. There may be other changes as well, such as converting inedible carbohydrate into an eatable form, or adding sugar to taste.

Branded items may also be quoted using these measurements, but in many cases it is more useful to quote by pack or portion size, as that is what you will actually be eating. In some cases food manufacturers have not given all the information we would have liked; as a result, inconsistencies in their labelling information are sometimes reflected in the tables.

Methods of Weight Control

Under normal conditions we are used to a varied and interesting range of foods. In fact, quite apart from the considerations of weight, it is only by having a varied diet that we can be sure to have the right mixture and quantities of all the other nutrients our bodies need. An ideal weight-reducing diet retains this variety, but reduces the incidence of high energy content foods — indeed, if permanent results are wanted, you should hardly realize that you are on a diet.

The first thing to do is consult your doctor. He or she will check over your medical history to ensure that the reason for your over-weight is simply over-consumption and not some more serious underlying condition. You must also see your doctor if you are pregnant or have recently had a child. Similarly if you have had or think you may have a heart condition, do not diet without medical advice. Plump children who have become much too fat for their own good must also let the doctor determine the best course of action.

The Low-Calorie Diet

This is the most basic and reliable plan available. You set yourself a given energy intake for each day (measured in calories) and stick to it until you reach your target weight. When you are your ideal size you then increase your calorie intake to just the level to keep your body fuelled throughout its day's activities.

There are two targets to go for: the 1500-calorie and 1000-calorie limits. The 1500-calorie plan is best suited to you if:

- you are used to big meals and would be inclined to cheat if you had less to eat;
- you lead a relatively active physical life;
- you have a great deal of weight to lose and need to pace your slimming carefully if you are to have any success.

The 1000-calorie plan is better if:
- you can cope with the idea of fairly small meals;
- you lead a reasonably passive life;
- your overall weight reduction programme is to lose no more than 15 kilos.

Don't try to go below the 1000 calorie limit.

You can of course set a 1200- or 1400-daily calorie level instead. On a daily 1200-calorie diet you should lose fat at the rate of about 1 per cent of your total body weight each week.

The psychological back-up you use is up to you. Some people are very self-disciplined and can keep a mental note of all the calories they have taken in. Others find it useful to keep a little notebook or diary. Others need the support of friends and family — or the confessional surroundings of 'Weight Watcher'-type groups where you are expected to 'tell' of any transgressions.

Other Diet Schemes
Some people prefer other dieting methods. Here are two frequently-touted alternatives:
The Low-carbohydrate Diet. The idea here is to count carbohydrates instead of calories — typically you are urged to limit yourself to 50 grams of carbohydrate a day. 50 grams of carbohydrate provides about 200 calories. Many foods contain no carbohydrate, and it is assumed that, by limiting your intake of carbohydrate, your intake of the other energy-providing ingredients will come up to somewhere between

1000 and 1500 calories a day. The advantage of the scheme is that there are fewer figures to manipulate and so the arithmetic is easier. The drawback is that the calculations can deceive. 50 grams of Cheddar cheese, the amount you might have with a cheese salad, contains no carbohydrate but has 12.7 grams of protein and 17.3 grams of fat – and will account for more than 200 calories!

The No-count Diet. This diet involves no counting, merely learning lists. It is easy but also very inflexible and likely to becoming increasingly inaccurate the longer a diet plan is supposed to last.

In Category 1 of this diet are foods you can eat as much of as you like: meat, poultry, game, fish, eggs, green vegetables, a few root vegetables, some fresh fruit, salads, and unsweetened tea or coffee. Category 2 is made up of foods to be eaten only in moderate quantities: milk, cheese, fresh fruit (the sweeter varieties), peas, beans, carrots, parsnips, etc., cream, butter, margarine and fats. The third category of foods are never (or only very rarely) to be eaten: sugar, sweets, chocolate, candy, alcohol, soft drinks, cakes and pastries, jam and marmalade, syrups, tinned fruit, crisps, nuts, fried foods, potatoes, pasta, bread and breakfast cereals.

Slimming Foods

There is no such thing as a 'slimming food' – one that will make you lose weight. Calorie-reduced prepackaged foods are usually traditional recipes made with low-calorie ingredients – bulky vegetables will be used instead of potatoes or rice, the 'mayonnaise' will be based on fromage frais, skimmed milk or processed whey rather than egg, lemon juice and oil, etc. There are also an increasing number of oil and fat substitutes, such as modified carbohydrates, dextrins, polyglycerolesters, polysaccharides, *Simplesse* from *NutraSweet* (an egg protein/milk protein/sugar product), oil/cereal/protein formulations, combinations of dextrin or protein with sucrose polyesters, carboxylate esters, polycarboxylic acid esters, esterified propoxylated glycerol and polysiloxanes. Whatever else they are, these new products are in no way 'natural'!

The most common artificial sweetener used to be saccharin, which can sometimes have a slightly bitter undertaste. These days increasing use is made of aspartame (NutraSweet), which has a much more acceptable taste.

Starch-reduced foods include certain breads, rolls and crisp breads. Special flour is used which enables more air to be pumped into the risen dough. The result is bread which looks as bulky as ordinary bread but weighs rather less.

Food bulkers are branded slimmers' foods which usually contain a fair amount of cellulose, so the stomach feels full without any calories being added. Some brands contain additional minerals and vitamins to overcome the problem of nutritional deficiency. You may also find 'quack' ingredients — herbs and the like for which unsubstantiated claims are made. Occasionally you will also find brands with laxatives in them — partly to counteract the constipation these diet foods can create and partly, it is alleged, to stop the stomach from retaining 'unnecessary' food. Laxatives should only be used under medical supervision or very occasionally and should not be part of any daily diet.

A few people do seem to find these 'slimming foods' useful, but many more get on perfectly well without them. They are usually very expensive in terms of what you get. Sometimes the very cost is supposed to be part of the 'treatment' — an added incentive to get the weight off and the diet over with!

There are also products available in some health food shops which are borderline drugs. Because they are technically 'food' they are subject to none of the important regulations which control the way in which medicines are offered for sale to the public. Nevertheless some of these products have very powerful and unexpected effects. There really are no safe short-cuts to controlling your weight; a 'natural' label doesn't make a dangerous quasi-pharmaceutical any safer.

Slimming Medicines
Do not use pills or other medicines unless prescribed for you by your doctor. Do not hunt around for doctors attached to special slimming clinics in the hope that they will give you miracle drugs that your own doctor would refuse to prescribe.

There are three sorts of medication sometimes suggested; the less reputable type of clinic sometimes offers pill cocktails, the blend being much more powerful than the individual constituents by themselves:

1. Drugs to make your stomach feel full; often bulking agents.
2. Fat-reducing drugs – sometimes pills, sometimes hormone injections.
3. Amphetamines. These make you feel less hungry and very energetic. They carry very unfortunate risks, including addiction or habituation and also other psychological side-effects.

> **The best method of weight control is the one that works – safely and permanently. A calorie-controlled diet should not be a temporary device to get you back to a 'normal' weight; it is for life.**

Bread

Fresh bread is 50 per cent carbohydrate. Nearly all this carbohydrate is in the form of starch, with sugars making up 2 to 4 per cent, depending on the recipe. Bread also contains 8 per cent protein, 2 per cent fat and 40 per cent water.

Toasting has the effect of reducing the water content in bread by about 20 per cent.

By the time bread has been fried it consists of only 8 per cent water; the energy nutrients then become: 8 per cent protein, 30 per cent fat and approximately 50 per cent carbohydrate.

Some bread doughs, for example those used for croissants, Indian naan and the Jewish cholla, have much higher levels of fat, which may have been introduced into the recipe either as butter or oil.

Apart from those doughs which contain significant amounts of fat, there is no cholesterol in bread.

Brown breads and those with added fibre are not, weight for weight, significantly lower in calorie than white bread, though of course they have other health benefits.

Crisp breads have had much of the water removed — typically they are under 10 per cent water as opposed to the 40 per cent in regular bread.

'Slimmer's Breads' usually have additional quantities of air or gas pumped into the dough during the baking process. The bulking up, of course, is supposed to induce the slimmer to eat less.

Effects of 'spreads': this is how you calculate the calorific value of a slice of bread or toast together with butter, margarine, jam, etc. (in grams):

- A 'thick' slice of pre-sliced bread is usually 40 to 45 g, a 'thin' slice is 25 g. If you cut your own bread, a thin slice will be about 40 g and a thick slice 50 to 55 g.

- A typical 'large' slice will carry 12 to 15 g of butter or butter-like spread: 90–110 calories of butter, about the same for margarine, and 45–55 for a low-fat spread. A typical coating of jam or marmalade would be 15 g, around 40 calories; a reduced-sugar jam would be 20 calories.

- A typical thick piece of toast (from a pre-sliced loaf) with butter and jam would be 250 calories – but, if the coatings were generous, it could be up to 330 calories. Two thin slices, each with the standard amount of butter and jam (or marmalade) would account for 400 calories!

- Most people put more butter/margarine on very fresh bread and on toast which is still hot.

Food Category or Brand	Calories /100 g	Portion	Size /g	Calories /port
Generic Breads				
bagel	270			
brioche	370			
brown	218			
brown rolls, crusty	255			
brown rolls, soft	268			
brown, toasted	272			
chapatis, with fat	328			
chapatis, without fat	202			
cholla	393			
ciabatta	259			
croissant	360			
currant bread	289			

Food Category or Brand	Calories /100 g	Portion	Size /g	Calories /port
currant bread, toasted	323			
French stick	270			
granary	235			
hamburger bun	264			
malt bread	268			
naan bread	336			
poppadums, fried	369			
pitta, white	265			
rye bread	219			
Vitbe	229			
white loaf	235			
white roll, crusty	280			
white roll, soft	268			
white, fried in lard	503			
white, fried in oil	503			
white, sliced	217			
white, toasted	265			
wholemeal	215			
wholemeal roll	241			
wholemeal, toasted	252			

Branded Breads

Allinson

100% wholemeal, medium slice		1 slice		75
100% wholemeal, small		1 slice		55
100% wholemeal, thick slice		1 slice		100
organic wholemeal, large		1 slice		75
soft wholemeal		1 slice		60
stoneground, large		1 slice		80
stoneground, small		1 slice		55
wholemeal grainstore		1 slice		75
wholemeal malt		1 slice		72

Food Category or Brand	Calories /100 g	Portion	Size /g	Calories /port
Asda				
bran crumpets		1 crumpet		70
butter croissants		1 croissant		185
crumpets		1 crumpet		75
garlic baguette		1 slice		60
wholemeal muffins		1 muffin		120
BN				
French toast		1 slice		30
French toast, wholewheat		1 slice		30
Champion				
rolls		1 roll		140
soft grain white		1 slice		85
Co-op				
crispbreads		1 slice		25
crumpets		1 crumpet		80
soft white baps		1 bap		145
soft white rolls		1 roll		110
wholemeal baps		1 bap		120
Country Pride				
crushed wheat, white		1 slice		80
Danish white		1 slice		50
Danish toaster		1 slice		60
traditional white, large		1 slice		80
traditional white, small		1 slice		65
Crofter's Kitchen				
oatmeal, large		1 slice		105
oatmeal, small		1 slice		70
Delba				
pumpernickel		1 slice		15
wholegrain rye		1 slice		60

Food Category or Brand	Calories /100 g	Portion	Size /g	Calories /port
Hovis				
Hovis bread	212			
Hovis bread, toasted	271			
golden bran		1 slice		80
golden oatbran, large		1 slice		85
granary malted, large		1 slice		80
granary malted rolls		1 roll		140
granary malted, small		1 slice		65
high-fibre wholemeal		1 slice		80
large white, medium slice		1 slice		75
large white, thick slice		1 slice		90
light wholemeal		1 slice		70
multi-grain, large		1 slice		80
organic stoneground, small		1 slice		60
stoneground wholemeal, large		1 slice		80
stoneground wholemeal, small		1 slice		60
wheatgerm, large		1 slice		85
wheatgerm, small		1 slice		65
wholemeal baps		1 bap		120
International Harvest				
croissants		1 croissant		185
mini croissants		1 croissant		145
mini white pitta		1 pitta		80
mini wholemeal pitta		1 pitta		70
naan		1 naan		390
white pitta		1 pitta		180
wholemeal pitta		1 pitta		160
Kingsmill				
large		1 slice		80
rolls		1 roll		125
small		1 slice		65

Food Category or Brand	Calories /100 g	Portion	Size /g	Calories /port
Mighty White				
rolls		1 roll		230
softgrain		1 slice		80
Mothers Pride				
Big T white		1 slice		115
brown baps		1 bap		140
burger buns		1 bun		140
croissants		1 croissant		220
crumpets		1 crumpet		80
Danish toaster		1 slice		65
Danish white		1 slice		50
light white		1 slice		55
long rolls		1 roll		110
morning rolls, white		1 roll		75
ploughman's rolls		1 roll		160
Scotch rolls		1 roll		130
Scottish batch		1 slice		120
traditional white, small		1 slice		65
white, long		1 slice		85
Nimble				
malty brown		1 slice		50
soft wholemeal		1 slice		50
white		1 slice		50
Olympus				
white pitta		1 pitta		185
wholemeal pitta		1 pitta		170
Safeway				
bran baps		1 bap		130
burger buns		1 bun		140
croissants		1 croissant		180
Danish		1 slice		50
mini pitta, white		1 pitta		80

Food Category or Brand	Calories /100 g	Portion	Size /g	Calories /port
mini pitta, wholemeal		1 pitta		70
mixed grain		1 slice		80
oatbran		1 slice		80
premium white		1 slice		80
Scottish rolls		1 roll		115
soft wholemeal		1 slice		65
softgrain white		1 slice		85
square		1 slice		115
stoneground wholemeal baps		1 bap		120
stoneground wholemeal rolls		1 roll		120
stoneground wholemeal, large		1 slice		80
stoneground wholemeal, small		1 slice		60
white pitta		1 pitta		180
white rolls		1 roll		105
white, sliced		1 slice		85
wholemeal		1 slice		80
wholemeal pitta		1 pitta		160
wholemeal rolls		1 roll		115
Sainsbury's				
baguettes, granary		1 baguette		290
baguettes, white		1 baguette		260
bloomer, brown		1 slice		85
bloomer, white		1 slice		67
brown crusty, large		1 slice		72
brown granary		1 slice		80
croissants		1 croissant		200
crusty rolls		1 roll		125
farmhouse		1 slice		72
granary malted, wholemeal		1 slice		90
granary wholemeal baps		1 bap		145
home bake baguette		half		130
mini pitta, white		1 pitta		90
mini pitta, wholemeal		1 pitta		90

Food Category or Brand	Calories /100 g	Portion	Size /g	Calories /port
morning rolls		1 roll		120
Nature's Choice, white		1 slice		55
Nature's Choice, wholemeal		1 slice		50
pitta, white		1 pitta		185
pitta, wholemeal		1 pitta		180
soft grain		1 slice		80
stoneground wholemeal		1 slice		75
wheaten		1 slice		75
wheatgerm Hovis, large		1 slice		80
wheatgerm Hovis, small		1 slice		60
white baps		1 bap		140
white salad baps		1 bap		165
white sandwich, large		1 slice		80
white sandwich, small		1 slice		60
wholemeal		1 slice		75

St Michael (Marks & Spencer)

Food Category or Brand	Calories /100 g	Portion	Size /g	Calories /port
bagels		1 bagel		210
brown rolls		1 roll		115
brown soda		1 slice		65
cracked wheat rolls		1 roll		85
dark rye		1 slice		95
garlic sticks		1 stick		20
grissini		1 stick		20
harvest brown		1 slice		55
hi-bran, large		1 slice		100
hi-bran, small		1 slice		55
oat bran stoneground, wholemeal		1 slice		60
oat flakes, white		1 slice		67
premium white		1 slice		80
ready to bake half baguette				245
sesame seed sticks		1 stick		20
soft grain		1 slice		80
stoneground wholemeal		1 slice		75
white cob		1 cob		135

Food Category or Brand	Calories /100 g	Portion	Size /g	Calories /port
white rolls, crusty		1 roll		105
white sandwich		1 slice		80
wholemeal		1 slice		50
wholemeal multigrain		1 slice		75
wholemeal sandwich		1 slice		75
Sunblest				
bloomer		1 slice		70
brown, long		1 slice		75
crusty cob		1 cob		150
Danish white		1 slice		40
farmhouse baps		1 bap		135
soft brown rolls		1 roll		120
soft white rolls		1 roll		115
split tin		1 slice		70
white, long		1 slice		80

Branded Slimmers' Breads

Hovis				
light wholemeal		1 slice		70
Mothers Pride				
light white		1 slice		55
St Michael (Marks & Spencer)				
lite malted brown		1 slice		50
lite white		1 slice		55
lite wholemeal		1 slice		50
Slimcea				
brown		1 slice		45
white		1 slice		45
Weight Watchers				
brown or white		1 slice		30
brown or white rolls		1 roll		100
Danish brown		1 slice		40
Danish white		1 slice		45

Food Category or Brand	Calories /100 g	Portion	Size /g	Calories /port

Branded Crispbreads

Co-op
savoury wheat   each   25

Kavli

crispbread wafer	each			20
harvest	each			40
high-bake	each			25
muesli	each			25

Living Foods
rice cakes, all flavours   each   25

Lyons

Krispen, rye	each			15
Krispen, standard	each			15
Slice-a-rice	each			25

Norsen
bran & sesame rye   each   25

Olof
golden Sweden crisp   each   20

Rakusens

Hilo	each			15
rye matzo	each			15
Superfine cracker	each			70
tea matzo	each			15
wheaten matzo	each			15

Ry-King

brown	each			35
fibre plus	each			30
golden	each			35
wheat plus	each			50

Food Category or Brand	Calories /100 g	Portion	Size /g	Calories /port
Ryvita				
brown		each		25
crackerbread		each		20
high-fibre		each		25
high-fibre crackerbread		each		15
original		each		25
sesame seed		each		30
Sainsbury's				
Krispwheat		each		20
wholemeal Krispwheat		each		15
wholemeal rye		each		25
Scandinavian				
GG bran		each		10
Scanda crisp		each		20
Swedawheat				
original		each		55
toasted		each		55

Branded Slimmers' Crispbreads

Co-op				
light		each		25
Finn Crisp				
light rye		each		35
Gateway				
light		each		20
light wholemeal		each		15
Slymbread				
original		each		10
rye		each		10
sesame		each		15

Food Category or Brand	Calories /100 g	Portion	Size /g	Calories /port
wholemeal		each		10
Superdrug Supatrim light		each		20

Cakes and Biscuits

Cakes

A cake consists of between 50 and 70 per cent carbohydrate, 15 and 35 per cent water, 4 and 10 per cent protein and 5 and 30 per cent fat. The starch component of the carbohydrate may be as low as 8 per cent or as high as 30 per cent, and the sugars may vary from 30 per cent to 55 per cent.

Icing and cream fillings put up both the fat and sugar elements.

Depending on the recipe, the fats are principally either saturated or monounsaturated, with relatively low amounts of polyunsaturated.

Individual pastries covered in icing or sugar and with fillings, especially cream buns, will have the highest calorie count.

Biscuits

As for biscuits, most are 65–70 per cent carbohydrate, 5–10 per cent protein and 15–30 per cent fats. Coated and filled biscuits have a higher proportion of fat and a correspondingly lower proportion of protein. The highest proportion of fats will be saturated, though the amount varies from recipe to recipe.

Food Category or Brand	Calories /100 g	Portion	Size /g	Calories /port
Generic Cakes				
battenburg	370	1 slice	80	296
cheesecake	492	1 slice	125	613
cherry cake	454	1 slice	125	565
chocolate cake	497	1 portion	100	497
coconut cakes	444	1 cake	80	355
cupcakes (iced)	356	1 cake	50	180
currant buns	305	1 bun	80	245
currant cake	418	1 portion	100	418
devil's food (iced)	337	1 portion	100	337
doughnuts	335	1 portion	100	335
Dundee cake	389	1 portion	100	389
Eccles cakes	518	1 cake	60	310
fruit cake	378	1 slice	125	470
ginger bread	381	1 slice	85	325
Madeira cake	393	1 slice	85	326
orange cake (iced)	469	1 slice	100	470
orange cake (plain)	465	1 slice	100	465
queens cakes	455	1 cake	75	315
rock cakes	419	1 cake	70	290
scones	369	1 scone	60	220
spongecake	308	1 slice	125	385
Swiss roll, chocolate	337	1 cake	75	253
Victoria sandwich	473	1 slice	125	590
Welsh cheesecake	489	1 cake	100	489
Branded Cakes				
Asda				
Bramley apple		1 cake		195
Eccles cake		1 cake		190
jam tart		1 tart		160
milk chocolate Jaffa ripple		1 cake		85

Food Category or Brand	Calories /100 g	Portion	Size /g	Calories /port
Birds Eye				
dairy cream eclair		1 cake		140
mini circle		1 cake		60
Cadbury's				
SMALL CAKES				
chocolate mini roll		1 roll		115
flake cake		1 cake		100
jam mini roll		1 roll		115
LARGE CAKES				
black cherry gateau		1 cake		368
chocolate cake		1 cake		282
chocolate Swiss roll		1 cake		232
Swiss gateau		1 cake		275
Lyons Bakery				
SMALL CAKES				
apple pie		1 pie		190
blackcurrant & apple pie		1 pie		200
caramel treat		1 cake		105
cherry Bakewell		1 cake		185
chocolate cupcake		1 cake		130
chocolate vanilla roll		1 roll		110
classic roll		1 roll		120
coconut crunch cake		1 cake		135
farmhouse slice		1 cake		115
fruit puff		1 cake		95
golden midi roll		1 roll		140
iced tart		1 tart		155
jam tart		1 tart		140
lemon curd tart		1 tart		150
lemon meringue		1 cake		150
strawberry fancy		1 cake		125
sultana apple slice		1 cake		150

Food Category or Brand	Calories /100 g	Portion	Size /g	Calories /port
toffee cupcake		1 cake		125
trifle sponge		1 cake		75
LARGE CAKES				
battenburg		1 cake		975
buttercream sandwich		1 cake		875
chocolate fudge		1 cake		1085
chocolate sandwich		1 cake		855
chocolate Swiss roll		1 roll		620
flan case		1 cake		460
French sandwich		1 cake		890
ginger		1 cake		1015
marmalade		1 cake		1260
raspberry Swiss roll		1 roll		510
Seville sponge sandwich		1 cake		1220
strawberry continental		1 cake		880
sultana		1 cake		975

Mr Kipling
SMALL CAKES

Food Category or Brand	Calories /100 g	Portion	Size /g	Calories /port
all-butter shortie		1 cake		145
almond slice		1 cake		140
apple & blackcurrant slice		1 cake		135
apple & custard pie		1 pie		205
assorted fruit crumble		1 cake		175
Bakewell slice		1 cake		160
battenburg treat		1 cake		155
blackberry & custard pie		1 pie		215
blackcurrant sundae		1 cake		185
caramel shortcake		1 cake		160
cherry Bakewell		1 cake		200
cherry slice		1 cake		130
chocolate fudge slice		1 cake		135
coconut macaroon		1 cake		105

Food Category or Brand	Calories /100 g	Portion	Size /g	Calories /port
French fancies		1 cake		100
harlequins		1 cake		145
Jaffa finger		1 cake		135
jam tart		1 tart		125
mince pie		1 pie		205
rich chocolate slice		1 cake		135
strawberry shortcake		1 cake		160
summer fruit pie		1 pie		185
LARGE CAKES				
angel layer		1 cake		364
apple & blackberry Bakewell		1 cake		361
Bakewell tart		1 cake		418
Bramley apple		1 cake		332
chocolate fudge		1 cake		386
chocolate Swiss roll		1 cake		332
jam Swiss roll		1 cake		214
lattice treacle tart		1 cake		353
Madeira		1 cake		328
Manor House		1 cake		428

Safeway

SMALL CAKES				
almond finger		1 cake		175
chocolate or orange mini roll		1 roll		125
frangipane		1 cake		235
meringue nest		1 cake		55
mince pie		1 pie		215
mini Yule log		1 cake		120
sponge finger		1 cake		25
trifle sponge		1 cake		80
vegetarian mince pie		1 pie		215
Viennese whirl		1 cake		220

Food Category or Brand	Calories /100 g	Portion	Size /g	Calories /port
Sainsbury's				
SMALL CAKES				
apple dessert tart		1 tart		295
blackberry & apple tart		1 tart		300
blackcurrant sundae		1 cake		175
Bramley apple pie		1 pie		195
chocolate cupcake		1 cake		130
coconut macaroon		1 cake		125
Danish pastry		1 cake		360
flapjack		1 cake		120
fondant fancy		1 cake		90
jam tart		1 tart		135
meringue nest		1 cake		45
mince pie		1 pie		200
treacle tart		1 tart		145
LARGE CAKES				
banana & coconut		1 cake		400
battenburg		1 cake		364
carrot, lemon cream		1 cake		386
chocolate chip & orange		1 cake		386
chocolate chip bar		1 cake		1320
chocolate-flavour Swiss roll		1 cake		375
Dundee		1 cake		339
ginger		1 cake		318
iced fruit		1 cake		339
Madeira, lemon iced		1 cake		379
spiced fruit		1 cake		375
treacle tart		1 cake		361
wholemeal carrot & orange		1 cake		368
wholemeal honey & fruit		1 cake		239

Food Category or Brand	Calories /100 g	Portion	Size /g	Calories /port

St Michael (Marks & Spencer)

SMALL CAKES

Food		Portion		Calories
assorted fruit sundae		1 cake		170
Bakewell slice		1 slice		160
caramel biscuit cake		1 cake		270
carrot & orange slice		1 cake		75
chocolate coconut finger		1 cake		150
chorley		1 cake		290
choux buns		1 bun		235
corn crisp		1 cake		130
dairy cream slice		1 cake		305
mince pie		1 pie		210
egg custard tart		1 tart		240
fondant fancy		1 cake		110
fresh cream meringue		1 cake		135
meringue nest		1 cake		60
rice crisp, raisins		1 cake		80
ring doughnut		1 cake		180
vanilla slice		1 cake		390
Viennese fancy		1 cake		190
walnut slice		1 cake		120

LARGE CAKES

Food		Portion		Calories
angel sandwich		1 cake		389
apple sponge sandwich		1 cake		282
apricot Swiss roll		1 cake		361
cherry Madeira		1 cake		375
chocolate-covered cake		1 cake		421
chocolate-covered roll		1 cake		411
clown		1 cake		404
coconut & cherry		1 cake		371
congratulations cake		1 cake		354
country		1 cake		454
Jamaica ginger		1 cake		386

Food Category or Brand	Calories /100 g	Portion	Size /g	Calories /port
parkin		1 cake		350
rich fruit		1 cake		375
sultana & cherry		1 cake		404
walnut sandwich		1 cake		407
Sara Lee				
chocolate fudge nut gateau		1 cake		1410
Tesco				
SMALL CAKES				
American muffin		1 cake		265
Belgian bun		1 bun		370
cherry Bakewell		1 cake		190
chocolate profiterole		1 cake		90
chocolate eclair		1 cake		330
corn crisp		1 cake		115
egg custard tart		1 tart		190
lemon curd tart		1 tart		160
sponge finger		1 cake		20

Generic Biscuits

chocolate digestive	493			
chocolate, full-coated	524			
cream crackers	440			
digestive	471			
flapjacks	484			
gingernut	456			
Jaffa cakes	363			
oatcakes	441			
sandwich biscuits	513			
semi-sweet	457			
shortbread	498			
wafer, filled	535			

Food Category or Brand	Calories /100 g	Portion	Size /g	Calories /port

Branded Biscuits

Asda

all butter shortbread		1 biscuit		100
almond & cherry cream		1 biscuit		70
almond shortie		1 biscuit		40
coffee & walnut cream		1 biscuit		70
digestive		1 biscuit		80
Garibaldi		1 biscuit		35
ginger nut		1 biscuit		45
ginger thin		1 biscuit		90
honey & bran crunch		1 biscuit		50
lemon crisp		1 biscuit		40
milk or plain chocolate digestive		1 biscuit		85
oat round		1 biscuit		70
orange crunch cream		1 biscuit		65
rich tea finger		1 biscuit		20
Scotch abernethy		1 biscuit		60
Scottish rough oatcake		1 biscuit		55

Boots

chocolate chip cookie		1 biscuit		80
coconut & cherry cookie		1 biscuit		85
custard cream		1 biscuit		65
digestive		1 biscuit		30
digestive cream		1 biscuit		60
ginger finger		1 biscuit		35
Nice		1 biscuit		30

Burton's

Bourbon		1 biscuit		60
chocolate chip & hazelnut		1 biscuit		55
coconut		1 biscuit		50
coconut cream		1 biscuit		60
coconut crisp		1 biscuit		35

Food Category or Brand	Calories /100 g	Portion	Size /g	Calories /port
coconut delight		1 biscuit		110
country snapjack		1 biscuit		80
fruit snapjack		1 biscuit		70
ginger nut		1 biscuit		45
Jaffa cake		1 biscuit		40
Jammie Dodger		1 biscuit		85
Rich Tea		1 biscuit		45
shortcake		1 biscuit		50
strawberry cream		1 biscuit		60
Viscount		1 biscuit		90
Wagon Wheel		1 biscuit		170
Wagon Wheelie		1 biscuit		90
Cadbury's				
Bournville digestive		1 biscuit		45
butter shortie		1 biscuit		45
chocolate orange digestive		1 biscuit		45
cookie		1 biscuit		50
hazelnut wafer		1 biscuit		45
orange cream		1 biscuit		80
Farmhouse				
chocolate fruit ginger		1 biscuit		75
chocolate shortbread		1 biscuit		75
coconut drop		1 biscuit		90
currant Shrewsbury		1 biscuit		65
farmhouse oat		1 biscuit		65
Melting Moment		1 biscuit		75
mild ginger		1 biscuit		75
shortbread		1 biscuit		145
Shrewsbury		1 biscuit		70
wholemeal square		1 biscuit		85
Fortt's				
Bath Oliver		1 biscuit		50
chocolate Oliver		1 biscuit		90

Food Category or Brand	Calories /100 g	Portion	Size /g	Calories /port
Fox's				
brandy snap		1 biscuit		55
chocolate coated ginger		1 biscuit		35
chocolate crunch cream		1 biscuit		60
Classic		1 biscuit		125
classic biscuit		1 biscuit		45
coconut crunch cream		1 biscuit		70
finger cream		1 biscuit		50
ginger crunch cream		1 biscuit		60
ginger snap		1 biscuit		35
golden crunch cream		1 biscuit		70
milk chocolate classic		1 biscuit		55
Morning Coffee		1 biscuit		25
petite beurre		1 biscuit		35
treacle		1 biscuit		80
treacle crunch cream		1 biscuit		65
triple		1 biscuit		100
McVities				
Abbey Crunch		1 biscuit		45
Boaster		1 biscuit		95
chocolate Hob Nob, milk & plain		1 biscuit		80
chocolate Homewheat, milk & plain		1 biscuit		85
Choice wholemeal		1 biscuit		60
digestive		1 biscuit		75
digestive cream		1 biscuit		60
fruit shortcake		1 biscuit		50
ginger nut		1 biscuit		45
Hob Nob		1 biscuit		70
Hob Nob Bar		1 biscuit		145
Jaffa Cake		1 biscuit		45
Jasper		1 biscuit		65
Lincoln		1 biscuit		40
Rich Tea		1 biscuit		35

Food Category or Brand	Calories /100 g	Portion	Size /g	Calories /port
shortbread		1 biscuit		105
Nisa				
Bourbon		1 biscuit		70
chocolate sandwich		1 biscuit		130
chocolate shortcake		1 biscuit		95
coconut ring		1 biscuit		40
cream cracker		1 biscuit		35
fruit shortcake		1 biscuit		35
ginger nut		1 biscuit		45
shortcake		1 biscuit		65
Peak Frean				
Bourbon		1 biscuit		60
coconut mallow		1 biscuit		50
custard cream		1 biscuit		55
Devon cream		1 biscuit		60
Marie		1 biscuit		30
milk or orange mallow		1 biscuit		55
Neapolitan wafer		1 biscuit		30
shortcake		1 biscuit		50
Safeway				
all butter thin		1 biscuit		25
almond shortbread		1 biscuit		90
coffee & walnut cream		1 biscuit		65
jam sandwich cream		1 biscuit		75
oaten crunch		1 biscuit		40
orange finger cream		1 biscuit		65
petticoat tail		1 biscuit		50
wholemeal honey sandwich		1 biscuit		75
Sainsbury's				
all butter biscuit		1 biscuit		40
all butter chocolate chip shortbread		1 biscuit		100
all butter crunch		1 biscuit		30

Food Category or Brand	Calories /100 g	Portion	Size /g	Calories /port
carob coconut finger		1 biscuit		85
chocolate teacake		1 biscuit		50
coconut cookie		1 biscuit		50
coconut crumble cream		1 biscuit		65
deluxe stem ginger		1 biscuit		85
fig roll		1 biscuit		65
fruit 'n' nut cream		1 biscuit		60
fruit Rustic		1 biscuit		70
Italian hazelnut cream		1 biscuit		90
jam mallow		1 biscuit		55
lemon puff		1 biscuit		75
milk chocolate Nice		1 biscuit		50
mint sandwich		1 biscuit		125
pink wafer sandwich		1 biscuit		30
thistle shortbread		1 biscuit		105

St Michael (Marks & Spencer)

almond		1 biscuit		45
brandy snap		1 biscuit		25
butter pecan cookie		1 biscuit		130
chocolate & black cherry		1 biscuit		50
chocolate cookie		1 biscuit		85
chocolate curl		1 biscuit		35
coconut finger		1 biscuit		70
lemon cream		1 biscuit		60
milk chocolate honeycombe		1 biscuit		125
milk chocolate toffee shortcake		1 biscuit		80
piped ginger shortcake		1 biscuit		60
sultana cookie		1 biscuit		80

Walkers

chocolate chip hazelnut		1 biscuit		90
hazelnut round		1 biscuit		95
honey & oatmeal		1 biscuit		85
muesli		1 biscuit		80

Food Category or Brand	Calories /100 g	Portion	Size /g	Calories /port
shortbread round		1 biscuit		90
stem ginger shortbread		1 biscuit		70
sultana		1 biscuit		80
treacle		1 biscuit		90

Cereals

The most popular breakfast cereals are made from corn, oats, wheat or rice, which are then heavily processed. Almost the entire energy content is in the form of carbohydrate and sugars. In the case of some of the cereal products aimed at children, over a third of the weight of the dried product is added sugar.

Mueslis and other cereals containing nuts will contain significant amounts of vegetable fat, up to 9 or 10 per cent. The deluxe (and hence more expensive) mueslis have more nuts and thus end up, weight for weight, with higher calorific values. Swiss-style mueslis may contain dried skimmed milk or whey powder.

Granolas are based on crunchy oats; the crunchiness comes from sugar-roasting the oats in oil, and this is why their calorific value is so high – the sugar content may be the equivalent of more than three teaspoons-full!

The figures given below are for the dry products. Assuming the addition of just under half a pint of regular milk, you will be adding a further 60 calories per serving; if you use skimmed milk, the addition will be about 30 calories, with semi-skilled it will be about 40 calories; if you sprinkle on a couple of tablespoons of sugar, you are adding a further 100 to 120 calories.

Cereal bars are listed in the **Sugar, Syrups, Confectionery and Cereal Bars** section.

Food Category or Brand	Calories /100 g	Portion	Size /g	Calories /port
Branded Cereals				
Allinson				
Bran Muesli	328	1 serving	30	98
Bran Plus	219	1 serving	30	66
Breakfast Muesli	354	1 serving	30	106
Boots				
high-fibre porridge	335	1 serving	30	101
honey muesli	417	1 serving	30	125
muesli (no sugar)	362	1 serving	30	109
Co-op				
chocolate chip muesli	404	1 serving	30	121
frosted cornflakes	393	1 serving	30	118
honey nut flakes	396	1 serving	30	119
Swiss-style muesli	389	1 serving	30	117
wheatflakes	364	1 serving	30	109
wholewheat muesli	379	1 serving	30	114
Granose				
Crunchy Nut	493	1 serving	30	148
Fruit Bran	302	1 serving	30	91
Soya Bran	93	1 serving	30	28
Wholegrain Fruit Muesli	408	1 serving	30	122
Holland & Barrett				
Bran & Apple Crunch	367	1 serving	30	110
Caribbean Crunch	390	1 serving	30	117
muesli, deluxe	214	1 serving	30	64
muesli, high-fibre	338	1 serving	30	101
muesli, sugar-free	380	1 serving	30	114
Jordan's				
Country Crisp	394	1 serving	30	118
Original Crunchy	356	1 serving	30	107

Food Category or Brand	Calories /100 g	Portion	Size /g	Calories /port
Kellogg's				
All Bran	211	1 serving	30	63
Bran Flakes	302	1 serving	30	91
Coco Pops	358	1 serving	30	107
Cornflakes	397	1 serving	30	119
Crunchy Nut Cornflakes	378	1 serving	30	113
Frosties	361	1 serving	30	108
Fruit 'n' Fibre	338	1 serving	30	101
Honey Smacks	346	1 serving	30	104
Rice Krispies	289	1 serving	30	87
Ricicles	364	1 serving	30	109
Sultana Bran	304	1 serving	30	91
Quaker				
Bran & Apple	425	1 serving	30	128
Oat Krunchies	383	1 serving	30	115
Puffed Wheat	325	1 serving	30	98
Quaker Oats	377	1 serving	30	113
Sultanas & Raisins	446	1 serving	30	134
Sainsbury's				
bran flakes	318	1 serving	30	95
coco snaps	351	1 serving	30	105
cornflakes	318	1 serving	30	95
hot oat cereal	368	1 serving	30	110
hot oat cereal (bran)	368	1 serving	30	110
rice pops	351	1 serving	30	105
sultana bran	301	1 serving	30	90
St Michael (Marks & Spencer)				
breakfast special	386	1 serving	30	116
chocolate flake muesli	446	1 serving	30	134
crunchy oat	425	1 serving	30	128
luxury fruit & flake	329	1 serving	30	99
strawberry muesli	436	1 serving	30	131

Food Category or Brand	Calories /100 g	Portion	Size /g	Calories /port
Tesco				
bran flakes	336	1 serving	30	101
cocoa puffs	357	1 serving	30	107
corn flakes	343	1 serving	30	103
golden puffs	361	1 serving	30	108
Waitrose				
bran flakes	340	1 serving	30	102
bran muesli	363	1 serving	30	109
cornflakes	345	1 serving	30	104
oat crunchy	390	1 serving	30	117
porridge oats	355	1 serving	30	107
rice crunchies	248	1 serving	30	74
wheat flakes	335	1 serving	30	101
Weetabix				
Alpen	375	1 serving	30	113
Alpen, no added sugar	371	1 serving	30	111
Alpen, tropical	379	1 serving	30	114
Weetabix		1 biscuit		65
Weetaflakes	368	1 serving	30	110
Weetos	393	1 serving	30	118
Whole Earth				
almond & orange crunch	414	1 serving	30	124
organic cornflakes	350	1 serving	30	105

Crisps and Snacks

All crisp products have about the same calorific value, 500 kcal/100 g. Approximately 50 per cent of a true potato crisp is starch and almost 40 per cent will be fats; the rest is protein. In a low-fat potato crisp, the fat content will be around 20 per cent, though there is no formal definition of what 'low fat' means. For example, there is almost no calorific difference between Sainsbury's Crinkle Cut (i.e. normal) crisps and its low-fat range, but KP's low-fat range are just under 400 kcal/100 g, 100 calories less than its 'normal' crisps.

Many 'potato' crisps are made from specially processed potato as opposed to actual slices of raw potato, and many are actually made of processed corn (that is, maize). The presence of corn is obvious in items like tortilla chips, but less so in the various 'crackers' aimed at children or the various pseudo-ethnic snacks from 'exotic' parts which may contain corn, processed potato and other flours.

'Mignons morceaux' are basically fried bread.

Many of these snacks contain significant amounts of salt — this may be important for people concerned with their blood-pressure.

Food Category or Brand	Calories /100 g	Portion	Size /g	Calories /port
Branded Crisps				
Co-op				
cheese puffs	578	bag	50	289
chip snacks	482	bag	50	241
crisps (all flavours)	529	bag	25	132
onion rings	522	bag	50	261
Streaky Crispies	476	bag	50	238
McCoy's				
beef	518	bag		207
cheese	523	bag		209
original	528	bag		211
Pringles				
light	511			
original	570			
sour cream & onion	571			
Sainsbury's				
Burger Bites	540	bag	50	270
cheese and ham nibbles	497	bag	33	164
chilli and mesquite flavour	495			
Cornitos	545			
crinkle cut crisps, ready salted		bag		211
Passanda Puri		bag		531
ready salted crisps		bag		134
salt & vinegar crisps		bag		208
savoury twirls with cheese		swirl		34
Safeway				
Carnival Mix	337			
cheese & onion	510	bag	25	128
cheese puffs	555	bag	50	278
crinkle cut, sour cream & chive	518	bag	25	130
Crunchy Sticks	469			

Food Category or Brand	Calories /100 g	Portion	Size /g	Calories /port
jacket crisps	486	bag	25	122
lightly salted	510	bag	25	128
potato sticks	517			
ready salted	534			
Savoury Twigs	391	bag	50	196
Trail Mix	495			
Tropical Mix	446			

St Michael (Marks & Spencer)

cheese squares	580			
cheese tasters	546			
cheese waves	512			
Indonesian crackers	541			
lower-fat crisps, salt & vinegar	482			
lower-fat crisps, beef	488			
Masala Puri	549			
Petit Pains	516			
pizza bits	543			
ready salted pipes	501			
salt & vinegar squares	461			
tortilla chips	476			
waffles	473			

Dairy Products

Milk

Milk is sometimes said to be the most nutritionally complete of all foods. Whole milk is 88 per cent water, 3 per cent protein, just under 5 per cent carbohydrate (in the form of sugars) and 4 per cent fat, two thirds of which is saturated fat.

In a *full skimmed milk* there is just a trace of fat, and the water proportion is 91 per cent. With *semi-skimmed milk* there is 1.6 per cent fat and just under 89 per cent water. Pasteurizing and homogenizing have no effects on any of these proportions, but in *sterilized milk*, some of the water content is lost.

In an *evaporated milk* the water content is down to 70 per cent, fat is up to 9 or 10 per cent, and protein and carbohydrate at about 8 per cent each.

Condensed milks are often sweetened. In condensed whole milk, the water content may be down as far as 25 per cent, fat at 10 per cent, but carbohydrate in the form of sugars up to 55 per cent.

Flavoured milks, for example with chocolate or fruit, will almost inevitably have additional carbohydrates in the form of sugars. There may also be additional fats.

Milk shakes are listed under **Drinks** (Non-alcoholic).

From a purely energy point-of-view, whole *goat's milk* is not significantly different from whole cow's milk.

The figures given for *dried milks* are for the undiluted powder and are rather misleading.

Soya milk isn't milk at all, but a liquid made from the soya bean. Other imitation milks are made from coconut oil and corn syrup.

Butter is listed in the **Fats and Oils** section.

Ice-cream has its own section.

Cream

Cream is the part of milk with the highest fat content. The main difference between the various creams offered for sale is the actual amount of fat.

Half cream has not less than 12 per cent fat and is almost 80 per cent water.

Single cream has at least 18 per cent fat.

Double cream is not less than 48 per cent fat.

Clotted cream is a minimum of 55 per cent fat and has the least amount of water — just over 30 per cent.

Sour cream has been soured with the aid of special bacteria and is usually based on single cream. *Crème fraiche* is fresh single cream treated with a culture to give a slight acidity. *Smetana* is single cream plus skimmed milk which has been carefully soured.

Buttermilk is the liquid cream left over after the cream has been used to make butter.

Yogurt

Yogurt is made from a mixture of whole milk, skimmed milk powder and sugars. 'Fat-free' yogurt is made with skimmed milk. Low-fat and fat-free yogurts will have a slightly higher carbohydrate and protein content compared with ordinary whole-milk yogurt.

Fruited yogurts often have additional sweetening quite apart from the sugars naturally occurring in the fruits.

A Greek-style yogurt contains much more fat than other types — up to 5 or 6 times more.

Fromage frais is a low-fat cream cheese made from curd;

its fat content depends on whether it has been made from
whole or skimmed milk. Yogurt drinks appear on p.115.

Cheese

Cheeses can be *hard* such as Cheddar and Parmesan, *soft*
such as Brie and Camembert, and *cottage*. The critical
difference from a nutritional point of view is the amount of
water they contain. Hard cheeses contain the least water,
cottage cheeses the most. In, terms of calories the hard
cheeses comes out at rather over 400 kcal/100 g, the soft
cheeses at about 300 and the cottage cheeses at under 100
kcal/100 g.

As you might expect, a 'full-fat' soft cheese has a high
proportion of fat. In a 'cream cheese' the fat content is almost
50 per cent.

Few cheeses have significant amounts of carbohydrate.

Eggs

The calorific value of 100 g of whole raw egg is between 145
and 165 kcal. By weight 75 per cent is water, protein
accounts for 12 per cent and fat 11 per cent. There is no
carbohydrate to speak of. If you are counting calories it is
always better to boil or poach eggs rather than frying or
scrambling them in butter or oil.

Food Category or Brand	Calories /100 g	Portion	Size /g	Calories /port
Generic Milks				
breastmilk, early (colostrum)	68			
breastmilk, late	78			
buttermilk, fluid	39	pint	284	110
coconut milk	53			
condensed	329			

Food Category or Brand	Calories /100 g	Portion	Size /g	Calories /port
condensed, unsweetened	154			
Crazy Milk, chocolate	63			
Crazy Milk, fruit	50			
dried, skimmed, powder	326			
dried, whole, powder	530			
evaporated	161			
Five Pints, reconstituted	46			
goat's	67			
long life, skimmed	34			
Marvel, dry	100			
Ostermilk, dry	453			
pasteurized whole	66			
semi-skimmed	46			
skimmed	35			
soya milk, sweetened	55			
soya milk, unsweetened	46			
spray-dried skimmed	51			
whole	70			

Generic Creams

aerosol cream	343			
brandy cream	436	carton	112	488
brandy cream, thick	440	carton	112	493
cherry brandy	425	qtr pint	112	476
clotted cream	579	qtr pint	112	648
double cream	461	qtr pint	112	516
double, with Cointreau	437	qtr pint	112	489
double, fresh	462	qtr pint	112	517
half cream	135	qtr pint	112	151
single cream	193	qtr pint	112	216
single, fresh	219	qtr pint	112	245
Smetana, regular	129	pint	284	365
soured cream	205	qtr pint	112	230
whipping cream	321	qtr pint	112	360

Food Category or Brand	Calories /100 g	Portion	Size /g	Calories /port
Generic Yoghurts				
diet types	52	carton	150	78
Greek	130	carton	150	195
low-fat, fruit	103	carton	150	155
low-fat, natural	60	carton	150	90
whole milk	62	carton	150	93
Branded Yoghurts				
Bailey's				
FRUIT BASKET				
extra creamy		carton	150	210
low-fat		carton	150	130
whole milk, fruit		carton	150	145
Boots				
CUSTARD STYLE				
apple & blackberry		carton		205
low-fat apple		carton		155
low-fat banana		carton		155
plum		carton		210
raspberry		carton		190
rhubarb		carton		195
GREEK STYLE				
apricot		carton	150	210
banana		carton	150	215
honey		carton	150	235
strawberry		carton	150	220
LOW-FAT				
apple & blackberry		carton	170	165
apricot & peach		carton	170	165
black cherry		carton	170	165

Food Category or Brand	Calories /100 g	Portion	Size /g	Calories /port
honey & hazelnut		carton	170	170
natural		carton	170	110
raisin & cinnamon		carton	170	155
strawberry		carton	170	165
THICK & CREAMY				
alpine strawberry		carton	150	170
apricot & mango		carton	150	170
fruits of the forest		carton	150	170
plum & apple		carton	150	165
raspberry & passionfruit		carton	150	160
toffee & hazelnut		carton	150	195
Chambourcy				
LE YOGHURT				
apricot & grapefruit		carton	125	105
pineapple & orange		carton	125	105
raspberry & lemon		carton	125	105
Dairy Crest				
VERY LOW FAT				
black cherry		carton	125	85
natural		carton	125	50
peach Melba		carton	125	90
raspberry		carton	125	90
strawberry		carton	125	90
THICK 'N' CREAMY				
exotic fruit		carton	150	175
rhubarb		carton	150	170
strawberry & vanilla		carton	150	170
Granose				
apricot		carton	125	90
blackcurrant & apple		carton	125	85
peach Melba		carton	125	90
strawberry		carton	125	85

Food Category or Brand	Calories /100 g	Portion	Size /g	Calories /port
Greek & Pure				
original		carton	240	350
Loseley				
apple		carton	150	145
apricot		carton	150	130
banana		carton	150	135
blackcurrant		carton	150	150
caramel		carton	150	170
hazelnut		carton	150	175
lemon		carton	150	150
mandarin		carton	150	140
natural		carton	150	100
pineapple		carton	150	145
raisin with rum		carton	150	155
strawberry		carton	150	130
Müller				
Crunch Corner	77	pot	175	134
FRUIT CORNERS				
kiwi & gooseberry	66	pot	175	115
peach & apricot	61	pot	175	106
Piedmont cherries	61	pot	175	106
strawberry	65	pot	175	114
Honey Corner	78	pot	175	136
LIGHT YOGURT				
peach & maracuya	46	pot	200	92
strawberry	47	pot	200	94
Safeway				
CUSTARD STYLE				
apple & blackberry		carton	125	180
rhubarb		carton	125	175
FRENCH				
all flavours		carton	125	95

Food Category or Brand	Calories /100 g	Portion	Size /g	Calories /port
FRUITS OF THE WORLD				
Brazilian		carton	150	145
Mediterranean		carton	150	140
Scandinavian		carton	150	140
Thai		carton	150	145
RICH & CREAMY				
apricot & mango		carton	150	180
kiwi & gooseberry		carton	150	180
orchard fruits		carton	150	175
peach & vanilla		carton	150	175
strawberry		carton	150	175
TRIMRITE				
banana		carton	125	60
black cherry		carton	125	60
fruits of the forest		carton	125	60
peach Melba		carton	125	60
raspberry		carton	125	55
strawberry		carton	125	55
Sainsbury's				
DIET DUET				
all flavours	50	pot	140	70
DUET				
apricot & peach	100	pot	175	175
red cherry	103	pot	175	180
strawberry	94	pot	175	165
three fruits	99	pot	175	174
St Michael (Marks & Spencer)				
CUSTARD STYLE				
blackberry & apple		carton	125	165
gooseberry		carton	125	165
rhubarb		carton	125	160

Food Category or Brand	Calories /100 g	Portion	Size /g	Calories /port
GREEK STYLE				
apricot		carton	125	170
honey		carton	125	190
natural		carton	150	195
strawberry		carton	125	175
LOW-FAT				
Bramley apple		carton	150	105
nectarine & orange		carton	150	125
raspberry		carton	150	110
William pear		carton	150	120
SET CREAMY				
apricot		carton	125	125
black cherry		carton	125	130
mango & apricot		carton	125	130
plum & raspberry		carton	125	125
strawberry & vanilla		carton	125	130
Ski				
ALPINE				
apple strudel		carton	150	140
chocolate praline		carton	150	140
mountain berries		carton	150	140
strawberry		carton	150	135
CLASSIC				
banana		carton	150	140
cherry		carton	150	140
hazelnut		carton	150	150
orange		carton	150	130
peach/pineapple		carton	150	135
raspberry/strawberry		carton	150	130
DIET				
cherry		carton	125	45
mandarin		carton	125	45

Food Category or Brand	Calories /100 g	Portion	Size /g	Calories /port
melon		carton	125	45
peach		carton	125	45
strawberry		carton	125	45
Total Greek				
with honey		carton	150	160
sheep's		carton	200	180
strained cow's milk		carton	200	270
Velouteta, any flavour		carton	150	190

Generic Fromage Frais

low-fat	45			
low-fat, fruited	45			
regular	110			
regular, fruited	133			
rich & creamy	120			
rich & creamy, fruited	150			

Branded Fromage Frais

Chambourcy

fruit, creamy	120	carton	100	120
fruit, very low fat	85	carton	100	85
natural, creamy	110	carton	100	110
natural, very low fat	50	carton	100	50

Safeway

apricot	135	carton	100	135
blackberry & raspberry	140	carton	100	140
exotic fruits	135	carton	100	135
strawberry	135	carton	100	135

Generic and Regional Cheeses

Appenzell	403	wedge	50	202
Austrian smoked	278	wedge	50	139
Babybel	343			

Food Category or Brand	Calories /100 g	Portion	Size /g	Calories /port
Bavarian Brie, mushrooms	393	wedge	50	197
Bavarian Brie, peppers	365	wedge	50	183
Bavarian, smoked	318	wedge	50	159
Beaufort	461	wedge	50	231
Beaumont	403	wedge	50	202
Bel Paese	343	wedge	50	172
Bleu d'Auvergne	346	wedge	50	173
Bleu de Gex	414	wedge	50	207
Bleu de Velloy	403	wedge	50	202
Bleu des Causses	382	wedge	50	191
Blue	366	wedge	50	183
Blue Brie	435	wedge	50	217
Boursin	404	wedge	50	202
Bressot	262	wedge	50	131
Brie	304	wedge	50	152
Caboc	554	wedge	50	277
Caerphilly	370	wedge	50	185
Cambozola	436	wedge	50	218
Camembert	309	wedge	50	155
Cantal	496	wedge	50	248
Chaumes	375	wedge	50	188
Cheddar	425	wedge	50	213
Cheshire	389	wedge	50	195
Cheviot	414	wedge	50	207
Chevret	303	wedge	50	152
cottage, uncreamed	388	portion	50	194
cream	813	portion	50	407
cream cheese, chives	439	wedge	50	220
cream cheese, natural	439	wedge	50	220
cream cheese, pineapple	386	wedge	50	193
curd	123	wedge	50	62
Danbo	346	wedge	50	173
Danish Blue	366	wedge	50	183
Danish Elbo	346	wedge	50	173

Food Category or Brand	Calories /100 g	Portion	Size /g	Calories /port
Danish Esrom	336	wedge	50	168
Danish Fynbo	361	wedge	50	181
Danish Havarti	439	wedge	50	220
Danish Maribo	368	wedge	50	184
Danish Mellow Blue	400	wedge	50	200
Danish Mycella	364	wedge	50	182
Danish Saga	461	wedge	50	231
Danish Samsoe	368	wedge	50	184
Danish Svenbo	382	wedge	50	191
Danish Tybo	325	wedge	50	163
Derby	403	wedge	50	202
Dolcellata	357	wedge	50	179
Double Gloucester	388	wedge	50	194
Edam	313	wedge	50	157
Edelweiss	393	wedge	50	197
Emmenthal	370	wedge	50	185
Etorki	478	wedge	50	239
Feta, Danish cow's	261	wedge	50	131
Feta, Greek ewe's	303	wedge	50	152
fondue mix	264			
full fat soft cheese, garlic, parsley	307	wedge	50	154
Gaperon	303	wedge	50	152
German, smoked	346	wedge	50	173
Gjetost	478	wedge	50	239
Gorgonzola	393	wedge	50	197
Gouda	340	wedge	50	170
Gouda, matured	390	wedge	50	195
Graindorge Livarot	328	wedge	50	164
Gruyère	465	wedge	50	233
Halali Limburger	261	wedge	50	131
Halumi	300	wedge	50	150
Jarlsberg	350	wedge	50	175
Lancashire	350	wedge	50	175

Food Category or Brand	Calories /100 g	Portion	Size /g	Calories /port
Langres	396	wedge	50	198
Leiden	407	wedge	50	204
Maasdam	475	wedge	50	238
Manchego	489	wedge	50	245
Mariolles	378	wedge	50	189
Mascapone	400	wedge	50	200
Melbury	325	wedge	50	163
Momolette	318	wedge	50	159
Morbier	375	wedge	50	188
Mozarella	279	wedge	50	139
Munster	328	wedge	50	164
Niolo	400	wedge	50	200
Norwegian Blue	357	wedge	50	179
Olivet	343	wedge	50	172
Orangerulle	328	wedge	50	164
Orkney	411	wedge	50	206
Orkney Claymore	396	wedge	50	198
Parmesan	420	sprinkling	5	21
Picodon	257	wedge	50	129
Port Salut	315	wedge	50	158
Primat des Gaulles	482	wedge	50	241
processed	374	wedge	50	187
Pyramide	350	wedge	50	175
Quark	88	wedge	50	44
Rambol with walnuts	418	wedge	50	209
Red Leicester	396	wedge	50	198
Red Windsor	407	wedge	50	204
Ricotta	146	wedge	50	73
Rigotte	350	wedge	50	175
Rollot	432	wedge	50	216
Roquefort	378	wedge	50	189
roule, garlic & herbs	329	wedge	50	165
roule, light	179	wedge	50	140
roule, spices	318	wedge	50	159

Food Category or Brand	Calories /100 g	Portion	Size /g	Calories /port
Royalp	393	wedge	50	197
Sage Derby	407	wedge	50	204
Sardo Pecorino	453	wedge	50	227
Shropshire blue	414	wedge	50	207
skimmed milk	82	wedge	50	41
smoked	390	wedge	50	195
Somerset goat's, natural	314	wedge	50	157
soya cheese	321	wedge	50	161
spread	290	spread	10	29
Sprinz	443	wedge	50	222
St Albray	343	wedge	50	172
St Ivel	380	wedge	50	190
St Nectaire	353	wedge	50	177
St Pauline	300	wedge	50	150
St Pecorino	453	wedge	50	227
Stilton, blue	418	wedge	50	209
Stilton, white	368	wedge	50	184
Taleggio	361	wedge	50	181
Tartare	443	wedge	50	222
Tartare, light	156	wedge	50	168
Tilsiter	418	wedge	50	209
Tomme blanche	400	wedge	50	200
Tomme grasse tourre	375	wedge	50	188
Torta	389	wedge	50	195
Vacherin Mont d'Or	339	wedge	50	170
Welsh goat's, herbs	307	wedge	50	154
Welsh goat's, natural	307	wedge	50	154
Welsh goat's, peppers	307	wedge	50	154
Wensleydale	406	wedge	50	203
Yarg	386	wedge	50	193

Generic Cottage Cheese

natural	102	1 carton	113	115
Cheddar-type	117	1 carton	227	265

Food Category or Brand	Calories /100 g	Portion	Size /g	Calories /port
Cheddar & onion	119	1 carton	113	135
chicken & mushroom	124	1 carton	113	140
fruit	117	1 carton	227	265
half-fat	84	1 carton	113	95
Mexican chicken	102	1 carton	113	115
onion & chive	95	1 carton	227	215
pineapple	97	1 carton	113	110
prawns	146	1 carton	113	165
salmon & cucumber	128	1 carton	113	145
spring onion	96	1 carton	225	215

Branded Cottage Cheeses

Shapers

gammon & pineapple	88	1 carton	113	100
natural	80	1 carton	113	90
pepper, sweetcorn & celery	75	1 carton	113	85
tuna & cucumber	84	1 carton	113	95

St Ivel Shape

Italian	71	1 carton	113	80
Mexican	71	1 carton	113	80
natural	71	1 carton	113	80
onion & Cheddar	95	1 carton	113	105
onion, chives & dill	66	1 carton	113	75
pineapple	71	1 carton	113	80

Primula

Cheddar spread	264
cheese spread	261
cheese spread, celery	257
cheese spread, chives	257
cheese spread, crab	257
cheese spread, ham	257
cheese spread, onion	253
cheese spread, pineapple	257
cheese spread, shrimp	257

Food Category or Brand	Calories /100 g	Portion	Size /g	Calories /port
Prewetts				
NON-ANIMAL RENNET				
Cheddar	421	wedge	50	118
Cheshire	378	wedge	50	106
Double Gloucester	386	wedge	50	108
Lancashire	371	wedge	50	104
Red Leicester	386	wedge	50	108
Eggs				
duck's	190	1 egg		115
hen's, dried	580			
hen's, fresh, whole	163	1 egg		80
hen's, fried	239	1 egg		70
hen's, in an omelette	172	1 egg		55
hen's, poached	160	1 egg		50
hen's, scrambled	172	1 egg		55
hen's, white	37	1 white		15
hen's, yolk	350	1 yolk		60
quail's	99	1 egg		15

Desserts

Most desserts are treats rather than contributions to a low-calorie diet. A range has been included so that you can see just how damaging they can be. For the slimmer, the ideal dessert is fresh, unsweetened fruit or some low-fat unsweetened dairy products (see the sections on **Fruits** and **Dairy Products**). Thereafter, almost everything is bad news: even plain stewed fruit is nearly always sweetened with sugar in various forms. Beyond that you are eating considerable amounts of pastry (flour, butter, eggs), other forms of complex carbohydrate, and cream and other high-fat dairy products.

There are separate sections on **Cakes and Biscuits** and **Ice-cream**.

Food Category or Brand	Calories /100 g	Portion	Size /g	Calories /port
Generic Desserts				
apple dumpling	202	1 portion	135	270
apple pudding	239	1 portion	135	320
apple pie	190	1 portion	135	255
banana custard	103	1 portion	135	140
blancmange	118	1 portion	135	150
bread & butter pudding	162	1 portion	135	220
canary pudding	462	1 portion	135	620
castle pudding, steamed	396	1 portion	135	530
chocolate mould	125	1 portion	135	170

Food Category or Brand	Calories /100 g	Portion	Size /g	Calories /port
custard powder (prepared)	116			
custard tart	290	1 portion	135	390
dumplings	206	1 portion	135	275
egg custard, baked	113			
egg custard, sauce	119			
gooseberry pie	180	1 portion	135	240
jam omelette	276	1 portion	100	275
jam roll, baked	403	1 portion	135	540
jelly, milk	111	1 portion	135	150
Leicester pudding	685	1 portion	135	925
meringue	393	1 portion	135	530
mixed fruit	325	1 portion	135	435
pancakes	301	1 portion	75	225
plum pie	183	1 portion	135	245
queen of puddings	213	1 portion	135	285
rhubarb pie	188	1 portion	135	250
rice pudding	144	1 portion	135	195
sago pudding	127	1 portion	135	170
semolina pudding	131	1 portion	135	175
suet pudding, plain	370	1 portion	135	495
suet pudding, with raisins	352	1 portion	135	470
syrup pudding	368	1 portion	135	490
tapioca pudding	129	1 portion	135	175
treacle tart	375	1 portion	135	500
trifle	150	1 portion	135	200

Branded Desserts

Ambrosia

apple/apricot rice	101	1 can	439	443
chocolate rice	103	1 can	438	449
creamed macaroni	92	1 can	439	405
creamed rice	91	1 can	425	385
creamed sago	81	1 can	439	355

Food Category or Brand	Calories /100 g	Portion	Size /g	Calories /port
creamed semolina	83	1 can	439	365
creamed tapioca	83	1 can	439	364
low-fat rice	74	1 can	425	315
traditional rice	103	1 can	439	450

Asda
black forest trifle	159	1 carton	113	180
caramel supreme dessert	129	1 carton	128	165
chocolate dessert, cream	135	1 carton	100	135
chocolate mousse	202	1 carton	62	125
chocolate sponge pudding	343	1 packet	300	1030
chocolate supreme	133	1 carton	128	170
creamed rice pudding	68	1 packet	213	145
fresh cream fruit trifle	137	1 carton	397	545
fruit trifle	155	1 carton	113	175
golden syrup pudding	293	1 packet	300	880
mixed fruit sponge pudding	327	1 packet	300	980
raspberry jam sponge pudding	283	1 packet	300	850
raspberry trifle	164	1 carton	113	185
rhubarb fruit fool	157			
strawberry mousse	145	1 carton	62	90
strawberry mousse, luxury	200	1 carton	80	160
strawberry supreme dessert	100	1 carton	128	128
toffee mousse	153	1 carton	62	95

Birds Eye
ANGEL DELIGHT
made with semi-skimmed milk		1 packet		380
with whole milk		1 packet		470
sugar free, semi-skimmed milk		1 packet		350
sugar free, whole milk		1 packet		440

Boots
banana fool		1 carton		220
black cherry delight		1 carton		150
Bramley apple fool		1 carton		215

Food Category or Brand	Calories /100 g	Portion	Size /g	Calories /port
fresh fruit salad		1 carton		55
gooseberry fool		1 carton		205
shapers chocolate mousse		1 carton		120
strawberry fool		1 carton		200
Brown & Polson				
DRY BLANCMANGES				
chocolate	335	1 sachet		136
custard mix	404	1 sachet		160
raspberry	330	1 sachet		125
Chambourcy				
black forest dessert		1 carton		140
cherry cheesecake		1 carton		215
chocolate crème Vienna		1 carton		150
pot au crème		1 carton		145
real chocolate mousse		1 carton		120
real crème caramel		1 carton		110
real fruit mousse		1 carton		105
strawberry cheesecake		1 carton		215
LE DESSERT CUP				
almond toffee		1 carton		155
chocolate coconut		1 carton		155
chocolate orange		1 carton		205
LE GRAND				
chocolate & vanilla		1 carton		270
strawberry & vanilla		1 carton		260
Chivers				
table jellies, all flavours	290			
FRUIT FOR ALL				
apricot	115			
blackcurrant	110			
morello cherry	110			

Food Category or Brand	Calories /100 g	Portion	Size /g	Calories /port
JELLY CREAMS				
chocolate	365			
other flavours	370			
Creamola (Dry)				
custard powder	354			
foam crystals, all flavours	323			
rice creamola	357			
steamed pudding mix	352			
Edenvale				
banana supreme	105			
blackcurrant cheesecake	207			
black forest trifle	152			
caramel supreme	127			
chocolate supreme	134			
chocomousse	180			
crème caramel	139			
crème orange	141			
crème raspberry	141			
fruit softy	129			
pear hélène sundae	132			
raspberry cheesecake	194			
raspberry trifle	153			
Spanish orange trifle	155			
strawberry cheesecake	196			
strawberry trifle	160			
tropical supreme	116			
Granose				
soya banana dessert	69	1 carton	525	360
soya chocolate dessert	89	1 carton	525	465
soya strawberry dessert	78	1 carton	525	410
soya vanilla dessert	79	1 carton	525	415

Food Category or Brand	Calories /100 g	Portion	Size /g	Calories /port
Heinz (Tinned)				
apple & blackberry sponge	265	1 can	300	795
chocolate sponge, chocolate				
sauce	297	1 can	300	890
mixed fruit sponge	298	1 can	300	895
raspberry jam sponge	285	1 can	300	855
strawberry jam sponge	287	1 can	300	860
treacle sponge	288	1 can	300	865
Weight Watchers rice	72	1 can	425	305
Homepride Mixes				
MICROBAKE				
chocolate pudding	328			
lemon pudding	319			
syrup pudding	330			
JUS-ROL				
apple slice		1 packet		140
apple strudel		1 packet		825
apple turnover		1 packet		145
butterscotch shell		1 packet		260
cherry slice		1 packet		130
lemon shell		1 packet		240
Lyons				
apple dessert pie		1 packet		1160
chocolate sponge pudding		1 packet		190
jam sponge pudding		1 packet		210
lemon meringue pie		1 packet		1415
McVitie's				
apple crumble	254			
apple dumplings	261			
apple pie	239			
chocolate & orange royale	289			
Chocolova	375			

Food Category or Brand	Calories /100 g	Portion	Size /g	Calories /port
Dutch apple tart	236			
jam roly poly	400			
nut meringue gateau	407			
profiteroles	475			
queen of puddings	207			
raspberry torte	275			
spotted dick	361			
strawberry pavlova	336			
tiramisu	329			
CHEESECAKES				
blackcurrant	396			
cherry	339			
chocolate truffle	386			
St Clements deep & creamy	343			
Milram				
chocolate crème	92			
hazelnut crème	104			
light & airy, all flavours	140			
vanilla crème	84			
Mr Kipling (Frozen)				
apple & blackcurrant crumble	264			
apple crumble	246			
golden syrup sponge	361			
rich jam roly poly	207			
spotted dick	354			
Müller				
low-fat rice desserts	70			
Nestlé				
custard powder, dry	330			
Double Top topping	178			
Tip Top topping	110			

Food Category or Brand	Calories /100 g	Portion	Size /g	Calories /port
Pearce Duff				
blancmange powder		1 packet		115
ice-cream mix		1 packet		320
jelly crystals		1 packet	50	185
sorbet mix		1 packet		375
sunnyfruit jelly		1 packet	95	320
Prewetts				
DESSERT WHIP (DRY)				
banana	440			
carob	445			
Ross				
apple dumpling		1 packet		335
black forest gateau		1 packet		1345
bread & butter pudding		1 packet		565
chocolate fudge		1 packet		1250
jam roly poly		1 packet		1360
lemon torte		1 packet		1450
pineapple pavlova		1 packet		1295
raspberry cheesecake		1 packet		2480
rhum baba		1 packet		350
spotted dick		1 packet		1250
Suisse delight		1 packet		1580
toffee apple pudding		1 packet		820
treacle roly poly		1 packet		1435
Rowntree				
jelly, all flavours	268			
instant custard mix, dry	416			
Safeway				
TINNED DESSERTS				
Christmas pudding	319			
Christmas pudding, luxury	327			
creamed rice	88			

Food Category or Brand	Calories /100 g	Portion	Size /g	Calories /port
jam sponge pudding	359			
rich fruit pudding	319			
semolina	350			
syrup sponge pudding	372			
traditional creamed rice	105			
FROZEN DESSERTS				
Banoffee pie	316	pack	430	1369
frozen yoghurt, all flavours	524	pack	275	1441
mousse, banana	163	pack	55	90
mousse, chocolate & mint	161	pack	55	89
mousse, raspberry	159	pack	55	87
peach melba gateau	242	pack	345	617
rhubarb crumble	189	pack	450	850
Sainsbury's				
apricot sensation		1 carton		100
banana cream		1 carton		145
black cherry double		1 carton		165
caramel surprise		1 carton		160
chocolate crème dessert		1 carton		150
chocolate mousse		1 carton		120
chocolate rice		1 can		460
chocolate surprise		1 carton		175
chocolate trifle		1 carton		280
coffee cream		1 carton		145
creamed rice		1 can		395
creamed rice, light		1 can		329
crème caramel		1 carton		130
fruit cocktail trifle		1 carton		160
gooseberry fool		1 carton		220
mousse, all flavours		1 carton		85
orange buttermilk		1 carton		130
pear buttermilk		1 carton		135
raspberry trifle		1 carton		115

Food Category or Brand	Calories /100 g	Portion	Size /g	Calories /port
rhubarb fool		1 carton		145
strawberry buttermilk		1 carton		135
strawberry fool		1 carton		185
strawberry trifle		1 carton		200
summer pudding		1 packet		495
FROZEN DESSERTS				
apricot fromage frais	174			
blackcurrant cheesecake		1 packet		1320
black forest gateau		1 packet		1230
cherry cheesecake		1 packet		1320
chocolate fudge cheesecake		1 packet		1490
chocolate fudge flan		1 packet		1680
cinnamon pastry bar		1 packet		1175
Danish pastry bar		1 packet		925
Hollywood passion cake		1 packet		1740
raspberry pavlova		1 packet		1260
red cherry fromage frais	151			
strawberry fromage frais	167			
strawberry gateau		1 packet		1320

St Michael (Marks & Spencer)

American-style sundaes,				
double choc chip	249			
apricot fool	162			
bramble fool	120			
bread & butter pudding	268			
butterscotch and toffee				
pudding	345			
fruit trifle	173			
orchard fruit tart	205			
Queen of Puddings	273			
rhubarb & redcurrant sponge	213			
strawberry fool	153			
syrup sponge	360			

Food Category or Brand	Calories /100 g	Portion	Size /g	Calories /port
summer fruit compote	99			
zabaglione	354			
FROZEN DESSERTS				
apple cream flan	215			
apple strudel	238			
apricot & peach pie	236			
chocolate cheesecake	377			
chocolate layer gateau	337			
chocolate pavlova	354			
chocolate russe	239			
deep and creamy tropical cheesecake	226			
frozen yogurt (all flavours)	73			
fruits of the forest cheesecake	217			
fruits of the forest gateau	221			
fudge flan	437			
lemon fromage frais cheesecake	221			
orchard fruit danish	247			
pecan danish	419			
raspberry pavlova	298			
Sara Lee				
raspberry fromage dessert		1 packet		810
Waitrose				
lemon mousse		1 carton		205
luxury chocolate mousse		1 carton		230
raspberry & redcurrant fool		1 carton		190
rhubarb fool		1 carton		155
strawberry fool		1 carton		170
FROZEN DESSERTS				
chocolate pavlova	296	1 packet	450	1330
exotic fruit tart	198	1 packet	440	870
lemon soufflé	253	1 packet	430	1090
summer fruit russe	262	1 packet	575	1505

Drinks

Alcoholic Drinks

The energy in alcoholic drinks comes partly from the alcohol and partly from sugars. One gram of pure alcohol provides the body with 7 kcal of energy.

An ordinary beer contains between 3 and 6 g of alcohol per 100 ml of fluid. (A half-pint is 280 ml, a common can size is 330 ml).

An ordinary cider contains just under 4 g of alcohol per 100 ml, but vintage cider might be over 10 g of alcohol per 100 ml.

For convenience the low- and no-alcohol versions are also included here rather than with the soft drinks that are listed in the 'non-alcoholic drinks' table. A no-alcohol beer will obviously have no calories from alcohol but is still likely to contain sugars.

Wines have between 8 and 10 g of alcohol per 100 ml.

Fortified wines — port, sherry and so on — are around 15 to 16 g of alcohol per 100 ml and 40-per-cent-volume spirits (the usual strength) are about 32 g of alcohol per 100 ml. Port may be up to 12 per cent carbohydrate (in the form of sugars) but some liqueurs, for example cherry brandy, may be over 30 per cent sugar.

The table below shows the relationship between an alcohol's strength — shown as percentage volume — and the weight of alcohol per 100 g of liquid. The figure on the far right is the calorific content of the alcohol; many of these drinks will have a higher actual calorific content, however, because of the additional sugars — a medium sherry, for example, may have 3.5 g of carbohydrate, pushing the calorific value per 100 g from 99.9 to 118.

Alcohol — Relationship between Percentage Volume and Calories

Drink	% vol	alcohol g /100 g	cal /100 ml
spirits	40	31.7	222.0
spirits	37.5	29.7	208.1
sloe gin	25	19.8	138.8
peach schnapps	23	18.2	127.6
freezomint	20	15.9	111.0
sherry	18	14.3	99.9
Bailey's	17	13.5	94.3
Taboo	14.9	11.8	82.7
Dubonnet	14.7	11.6	81.6
Sanatogen	14.5	11.5	80.5

Hot Drinks

By themselves, neither tea nor coffee have any calorific value — any sugar or milk added does. Each teaspoon of sugar is 20 calories. A dash of milk — say 30 ml — is another 20 calories. Most herbal teas similarly have no calorific value, but those infusions based on fruits may have inherent sugars.

Cocoa and chocolate-based drinks, and those with malt in them, may be based either on powdered whole milk or on semi-skimmed or skimmed milk. While some chocolate drinks simply require the addition of water, most of the older varieties expect you to add milk.

There is a separate **Soups** listing; however, at the end of the Hot Drinks table there is a section on the drinks and convenience soups sold from vending machines.

Non-Alcoholic Drinks

Nearly all commercially manufactured non-alcoholic drinks contain large amounts of added sugar or sweeteners. Fruits themselves are chiefly glucose and fructose, but apples and pears also include sucrose.

The packaging on fruit juices needs to be read with particular care: only the most expensive brands are solely 'juice' in the sense that you end up with the drink you would make at home by squeezing a piece of fresh fruit. Usually the flesh – and sometimes part of the skin – is pulped and heat-treated.

The fruits used in juices made 'from concentrate' are kept in concentrated form and then diluted when placed in the carton or bottle which you eventually buy.

Squashes are drink concentrates; you must divide the figures supplied in the table by the amount you dilute them.

Carbonation – injecting bubbles to produce a fizzy drink – has no direct effect on calorific value, but the process usually adds an acidic taste which the manufacturer then counteracts by adding sugars.

'Diet' and 'Lo-Cal' drinks use artificial sweeteners.

Glucose drinks such as Lucozade are made from glucose syrup and thus have very high calorific values – fine if you are an athlete or invalid, bad news if you are slimming.

This section also includes milk shakes, as opposed to flavoured milks, which are located in the **Dairy Products** section.

You will also find some soft drinks and milk shakes in the **Fast Foods** section.

Food Category or Brand	Calories /100 ml	Portion	Size /ml	Calories /port
Branded Beers				
Bass				
draught	36	1 can	440	16
Beamish				
canned	34	1 can	440	150
draught	32	½ pint	284	90
Bentley				
bottled	28	1 bottle	284	80
Burton's				
canned	41	1 can	440	180
draught	42	½ pint	284	120
Courage				
draught	35	½ pint	284	100
Double Diamond				
canned	38	1 can	440	165
draught	32	½ pint	284	90
Ind Coope				
bottled	27	1 bottle	275	75
draught	28	½ pint	284	80
John Bull				
draught	30	½ pint	284	85
John Smith's				
canned	36	1 can	440	160
draught	33	½ pint	284	95
London Pride				
draught	37	½ pint	284	105
McEwans Export				
canned	36	1 can	440	160

Food Category or Brand	Calories /100 ml	Portion	Size /ml	Calories /port
Newcastle Brown bottled	38	1 bottle	440	165
Ruddles draught	35	½ pint	284	100
Stones draught	32	½ pint	284	90
Tartan canned	31	1 can	440	138
Tetley canned	32	1 can	440	140
Walkers draught	28	½ pint	284	80
Watney's draught	33	½ pint	284	95
Webster's draught	32	½ pint	284	90
Worthington's canned	27	1 can	440	120

Low- and No-alcohol Branded Beers

Food Category or Brand	Calories /100 ml	Portion	Size /ml	Calories /port
LA Bitter bottled	24	1 bottle	275	65
John Smith's bottled	16	1 bottle	275	45
McEwans LA canned	15	1 can	440	65
Swan Light canned	17	1 can	440	75

Food Category or Brand	Calories /100 ml	Portion	Size /ml	Calories /port
White Label				
canned	31	1 can	440	135

Branded Lagers

Budweiser				
draught	39	½ pint	284	110
Carling Black Label				
canned	32	1 can	440	140
Carlsberg				
bottled	45	1 bottle	275	125
Castlemaine XXXX				
canned	38	1 can	440	165
Foster's				
canned	40	1 can	375	150
draught	32	½ pint	284	90
Heineken				
bottled	31	1 bottle	275	85
Hofmeister				
canned	30	1 can	440	130
draught	30	½ pint	284	85
Holsten Export				
draught	40	½ pint	284	115
Holsten Pils				
canned	39	1 can	440	170
Kestrel				
canned	26	1 can	440	115
Kronenbourg				
canned	42	1 can	440	185
draught	42	½ pint	284	120

Food Category or Brand	Calories /100 ml	Portion	Size /ml	Calories /port
Lamot Pils				
canned	38	1 can	440	165
Löwenbräu Pils				
canned	41	1 can	440	180
Skol				
canned	28	1 can	440	125
Stella Artois				
canned	42	1 can	440	185
Tennent's				
canned	32	1 can	440	140
draught	33	½ pint	284	95

Extra-strength Branded Lagers

Carlsberg Special Brew				
bottled	75	1 bottle	275	205
Kestrel Super Strength				
canned	75	1 can	440	330
Skol Extra Strength				
canned	70	1 can	440	310
Tennents Super				
canned	73	1 can	440	320

Low- and No-alcohol Branded Lagers

Barbican				
bottled	12	1 bottle	275	35
Carlton				
draught	18	½ pint	284	50

Food Category or Brand	Calories /100 ml	Portion	Size /ml	Calories /port
Miller Lite				
canned	27	1 can	440	120
draught	26	½ pint	284	75
Swan				
canned	19	1 can	375	70
Tennent's LA				
canned	18	1 can	440	80

Branded Ciders

Blackthorn				
dry, bottled	35	1 bottle	275	95
Copperhead				
canned	35	1 can	440	154
dry, draught	30	½ pint	284	85
dry, strong, draught	35	1 bottle	275	96
Country Manor				
medium dry, draught	55	½ pint	284	155
medium sweet, draught	63	½ pint	284	180
rosé, draught	46	½ pint	284	130
sparkling, draught	60	½ pint	284	170
Diamond White				
bottled	53	1 bottle	275	145
Merrydown				
country, draught	49	½ pint	284	140
traditional, draught	46	½ pint	284	130
vintage, draught	60	½ pint	284	170
vintage dry, draught	53	½ pint	284	150
Red Rock				
bottled	41	1 bottle	330	135

Food Category or Brand	Calories /100 ml	Portion	Size /ml	Calories /port
Strongbow				
draught	36	½ pint	284	101
Taunton Cool				
bottled	35	1 bottle	275	95
Woodpecker				
draught	35	½ pint	284	100

Generic Wines

champagne	70	glass	115	80
red, dry	70	glass	115	80
red, sweet	87	glass	115	100
rosé	74	glass	115	85
sparkling	78	glass	115	90
white, dry	65	glass	115	75
white, sweet	91	glass	115	105

Generic Fortified Wines

ruby or tawny	150	measure	50	75
port, vintage	160	measure	50	80
port, white	100	measure	50	70
sherry, cream	126	measure	50	63
sherry, dry	100	measure	50	54
sherry, medium	116	measure	50	58

Generic Spirits

brandy, apricot	240	measure	25	60
brandy, average	200	measure	25	50
gin	200	measure	25	50
rum	200	measure	25	50
vodka	200	measure	25	50
whisky	200	measure	25	50

Food Category or Brand	Calories /100 ml	Portion	Size /ml	Calories /port
Branded Spirits				
Bacardi	200	measure	25	50
Jack Daniels	240	measure	25	60
Martini				
Bianco	134	measure	50	67
Extra Dry	134	measure	50	67
Rosso	170	measure	50	85
Pernod	244	measure	25	61
Pimms	196	measure	50	98
Southern Comfort	280	measure	25	70
Branded Liqueurs				
Advocaat	260	measure	25	65
Bailey's Irish Cream	320	measure	25	80
Benedictine	360	measure	25	90
Cassis	260	measure	25	65
Cointreau	340	measure	25	85
Drambuie	340	measure	25	85
Grand Marnier	320	measure	25	80
Irish Velvet	380	measure	25	95
Kirsch	200	measure	25	50
Mardi Gras	200	measure	25	50
Tia Maria	300	measure	25	75

Food Category or Brand	Calories /100 ml	Portion	Size /ml	Calories /port

Generic Hot Drinks
tea, Indian	1			
coffee	2			

Branded Hot Drinks

Boots
malted drink		1 tsp		21

Bovril
		1 tsp		10

Cadbury's
Bournvita		1 tsp		22
Bournvita Break		1 sachet		110
Caramel Chocolate Break		1 sachet		90
Dark Mint Break		1 sachet		105
Drinking Chocolate		2 tsps		40
Highlights		sachet		40
Horlicks				
low-fat		sachet		129
low-fat chocolate		sachet		124
Marvel		1 tsp		6
Milk Chocolate Break		1 sachet		105
Plain Chocolate Break		1 sachet		105

Carnation
Build Up		1 sachet		130
Slim Chocolate		1 sachet		41
Tea-mate		1 tsp		10

Horlicks
Instant		1 sachet		105
Instant Chocolate Malted		1 sachet		125
Instant Hot Chocolate		1 sachet		130

Food Category or Brand	Calories /100 ml	Portion	Size /ml	Calories /port
Lift				
lemon tea		2 tsps		35
London Herb & Spice Co.				
Natural Break		1 cup		5
Nestlé				
cappuccino, original		cup		48
cappuccino, unsweetened		cup		47
Elevenses		1 tsp		5
Milo		1 tsp		24
Ovaltine				
Choc-a-coconut		1 sachet		40
Choc-a-mint		1 sachet		40
Choc-a-mocha		1 sachet		40
Choc-a-orange		1 sachet		40
Choc-n-banana		1 sachet		40
Choc-n-toffee		1 sachet		40
Choc-o-lait		1 sachet		40
chocolate-flavoured		2 tsps		10
granules		3 tsps		55
instant		1 sachet		120
instant drinking chocolate		1 sachet		135
Oxo				
beef drink		1 tsp		5
cubes, all flavours		1 cube		15
Sainsbury's				
duos, instant hot chocolate		sachet		39
malted drink		2 tsps		55
Superdrug				
Supatrim instant chocolate		1 sachet		40
Supatrim malted milk		1 sachet		40

Food Category or Brand	Calories /100 ml	Portion	Size /ml	Calories /port
Symingtons				
dandelion coffee		1 tsp		15
Typhoo				
QT instant white tea		cup		11

Vending Machine Drinks

Food Category or Brand	Calories /100 ml	Portion	Size /ml	Calories /port
Drinkmaster				
blackcurrant		1 cup		35
Bovril		1 cup		10
chicken soup		1 cup		40
chocolate-flavoured		1 cup		70
coffee, white, no sugar		1 cup		15
coffee, white, with sugar		1 cup		45
continental chocolate		1 cup		60
decaf, white, no sugar		1 cup		20
Five Star, white, no sugar		1 cup		25
French onion soup		1 cup		35
lemon tea		1 cup		40
tea, white, no sugar		1 cup		10
tomato & beef soup		1 cup		35
vegetable soup		1 cup		40
Maxpax				
blackcurrant		1 cup		25
Bovril		1 cup		10
chicken soup		1 cup		25
chocolate		1 cup		65
lemon tea		1 cup		35
malted drink		1 cup		55
Master Blend		1 cup		20
oxtail soup		1 cup		25
saccharin-free chocolate		1 cup		70
tomato soup		1 cup		20
vegetable soup		1 cup		25

Food Category or Brand	Calories /100 ml	Portion	Size /ml	Calories /port
Generic Fruit Juices				
blood orange	39	¼ pint	142	55
clementine	49	¼ pint	142	70
grapefruit	39	¼ pint	142	55
minneola	39	¼ pint	142	55
orange	32	¼ pint	142	45
orange & grapefruit	32	¼ pint	142	45
ortanique	39	¼ pint	142	55
pineapple	42	¼ pint	142	60
pineapple & grapefruit	49	¼ pint	142	70
pink grapefruit	42	¼ pint	142	60

Branded Fruit and Vegetable Juices

Boots

English apple	47
grapefruit	31
orange	33
tomato	16

Bulmer's

apple	37
grape	43
Kiri	37

Copella

apple	40
blackcurrant with apple	50
morello cherry with apple	37
pear with apple	40

Libby's

apple 'C'	45
blackcurrant 'C'	42

Food Category or Brand	Calories /100 ml	Portion	Size /ml	Calories /port
grapefruit	38			
grapefruit 'C', sweetened	58			
orange, sweetened	51			
orange, unsweetened	33			
orange 'C', sweetened	51			
pineapple	53			
tomato	20			
umbongo fruit	41			
Lindavia				
apple, clear	42			
apple, unfiltered	45			
apricot	60			
blackberry	29			
blackcurrant	56			
carrot	23			
cherry	55			
grapefruit	22			
orange	42			
passionfruit	34			
peach	37			
pear	45			
plum	64			
redcurrant	57			
red & white grape	63			
tomato	18			
vegetable	30			
Longlife				
apple & mango	46	¼ pint	142	65
English apple	39	¼ pint	142	55
mandarin	39	¼ pint	142	55
orange & apricot	46	¼ pint	142	65
red grapefruit	32	¼ pint	142	45

Food Category or Brand	Calories /100 ml	Portion	Size /ml	Calories /port
Prewetts				
apple & cherry	73			
grapefruit	40			
orange	43			
orange, banana & lemon	36			
vegetable (country blend)	27			
Safeway				
English apple	45			
orange	40			
pineapple	43			
Sainsbury's				
exotic fruit juice	40			
five fruits juice drink	50			
reduced calorie exotic fruits	15			
reduced calorie orange	15			
St Michael (Marks & Spencer)				
apple & mango	42			
blackcurrant	48			
Caribbean	43			
mandarin	37			
sunfruit	47			
Spar				
'8' fruit drink	44			
grapefruit	31			
orange	39			
pure apple	42			
'Saver' Breakfast Orange	41			
Volonte				
apple	40			
grapefruit	36			
orange	40			
pineapple	49			

Food Category or Brand	Calories /100 ml	Portion	Size /ml	Calories /port
red & white grape	60			
tomato	16			

Waitrose

apple	43			
apple & cherry cocktail	39			
English apple	43			
Five Fruit	52			
grape & blackcurrant	71			
grapefruit	30			
orange	35			
pineapple	43			

Branded Carbonated Drinks

Barr

Iron-Bru	40	1 can	330	132
Shandy	32	1 can	330	106
Tizer	40	1 can	330	132
Vimto	26	1 can	330	86

Britvic

ginger ale, dry	22	1 can	330	73
ginger beer	42	1 can	330	139
lime, lemon, orange	50	1 can	330	165
tonic water	31	1 can	330	102

Coca-Cola

caffeine-free Coke	0	1 can	330	0
Coca Cola	41	1 can	330	135
Diet Coke	0	1 can	330	0
Cherry Coke	42	1 can	330	140

Corona

cherryade	26	1 bottle	250	65
lemonade	24	1 bottle	250	60
orangeade	28	1 bottle	250	70

Food Category or Brand	Calories /100 ml	Portion	Size /ml	Calories /port
Fanta				
cream soda	28	1 can	330	92
ginger beer	31	1 can	330	102
lemonade	24	1 can	330	79
orangeade	33	1 can	330	109
raspberryade	29	1 can	330	96
sparkling lemon	35	1 can	330	116
Lucozade				
barley, lemon & orange	72	1 can	330	238
glucose	73	1 can	330	241
Isotonic Orange	26	1 can	330	86
Sport	11	1 can	330	36
Schweppes				
bitter lemon	33	1 can	330	109
bitter orange	44	1 can	330	145
ginger ale	22	1 can	330	73
ginger ale, dry	16	1 can	330	53
ginger beer	35	1 can	330	116
lemonade	25	1 can	330	83
lemonade shandy	26	1 can	330	86
orange	39	1 can	330	129
Russian	22	1 can	330	73
strawberry	36	1 can	330	119
tonic water	19	1 can	330	63
Tropical Spring	30	1 can	330	99
Tango				
apple	36	1 can	330	119
grapefruit	42	1 can	330	139
lemon with lime	35	1 can	330	116
orange	45	1 can	330	149

Food Category or Brand	Calories /100 ml	Portion	Size /ml	Calories /port
White's				
cherryade	20	1 can	330	66
cream soda	20	1 can	330	66
dandelion & burdock	25	1 can	330	83
ginger beer	29	1 can	330	96
lemonade	20	1 can	330	66
lemonade, traditional	28	1 can	330	92
orangeade	23	1 can	330	76

Branded Squashes (Concentrated)

Boots				
blackcurrant	205			
English fruit	202			
lemon barley	120			
lemon, honey & ginger	140			
orange barley	130			
tropical fruit	167			
Britvic				
blackcurrant	122			
high-juice lemon	128			
high-juice lime	134			
high-juice orange	128			
lemon	96			
orange	108			
peppermint	92			
Robinson's				
lemon barley	105			
lime juice	140			
orange barley	110			
original lemon	140			
original orange	155			

Food Category or Brand	Calories /100 ml	Portion	Size /ml	Calories /port
Safeway				
apple & rhubarb	140			
glucose health	80			
lemon	90			
lemon & lime	99			
lime cordial	99			
orange	94			
orange & apricot	98			
orange & peach	94			
pineapple & coconut	90			
raspberry	140			
St Michael (Marks & Spencer)				
blackberry & apple	221			
blackcurrant	172			
pear & raspberry	217			
Waitrose				
blackcurrant	229			
Caribbean	85			
lemon	87			
lemon & lime	85			
lime cordial	87			
orange, high juice	134			
orange, squash	104			
orange & peach	86			

Branded Milk Shakes

Breaktime				
banana	63	1 carton	200	125
chocolate	70	1 carton	200	140
strawberry	63	1 carton	200	125
Cadbury's				
chocolate milk	93	1 carton	200	185

Food Category or Brand	Calories /100 ml	Portion	Size /ml	Calories /port
Crusha Syrup				
banana	111			
black cherry	139			
chocolate	175			
lime	107			
pineapple	111			
raspberry	104			
strawberry	104			
toffee	164			
Dairy Crest				
banana	60	1 carton	200	120
chocolate	63	1 carton	200	125
strawberry	60	1 carton	200	120
Edenvale				
made up, all flavours	75	glass	150	113
Elan, Yazoo				
banana	65	1 carton	200	130
chocolate	68	1 carton	200	135
strawberry	65	1 carton	200	130
Mars				
milk drink	100	1 carton	200	200
Nestlé				
Nesquik with whole milk, all flavours	170	1 glass	150	
St Michael (Marks & Spencer)				
chocolate	86	1 glass	150	
Spar				
banana	50	1 glass	150	
chocolate	60	1 glass	150	
strawberry	50	1 glass	150	

Food Category or Brand	Calories /100 ml	Portion	Size /ml	Calories /port
Supershakes				
all flavours	75	1 glass	15	
Waitrose				
butterscotch	98	1 glass	150	
chocolate	73	1 glass	150	
fudge	98	1 glass	150	
strawberry	68	1 glass	150	

Yoghurt Drinks

Sainsbury's
black cherry/strawberry   70

Ski
strawberry   71

Yop
exotic fruits   79
vanilla   75

Ethnic Foods

These 'exotic' foods are the popular dishes you will find on many restaurant menus. It would have been preferable to include cuisines from rather more cultures, but nutritional data is scarce for the less common styles of cooking. Obviously each chef will make each dish slightly differently and restaurants vary considerably in the size of portions offered, so these calorific figures are 'indicative' rather than precise.

Various ethnic dishes, both chilled and frozen, are also available from supermarkets. You will find a range of these in the **Ready-made Meals** section.

You can often guess at the calorific value of an individual item if you know a little about the cooking method involved. Here are some generalizations about low-calorie choices for each form of popular cuisine:

- Chinese: avoid 'sweet-and-sour' type sauces and have plain, boiled rice rather than any other kind. Select simple stir-fried dishes, and meats that have been roasted or wind-dried.

- French: French sauces can contain large amounts of carbohydrate and fats. As a main course stick with those made with wine rather than cream or cheese sauces. Better still, look for simple grills. Choose clear soups rather than thickened ones. Ask for fresh fruit for dessert.

- Greek: Greek salads often have feta cheese; but this is still a better choice than taramasalata or houmous, which is made with olive oil. The charcoal grill is an important

part of Greek cooking and almost anything from that will
be relatively 'safe' — you can have fish as well as kebabs.
Moussaka has large amounts of dairy product in the sauce
and slimmers should avoid it. Almost all the Greek
pastries are very fattening as they are drenched in honey.

- Indian: the best slimmer's choices come from the *tandoor*,
  the clay oven from which you get chicken tandoori, tikka
  and seekh kebab. Of the various Indian sauces, madras is
  the most fattening. A lot of Indian cooking is done with
  ghee — clarified butter. The figures given for biriyani
  dishes may be misunderstood: a biriyani is a complete
  main course; the others are elements from which you
  make up your meal.

- Italian: on the whole, the Italian cuisine is not for those
  on a slimming diet. Look mostly for salads and simple
  stuffed vegetable dishes. The problem is not so much
  pizza and pasta themselves (tables for which are in the
  Rice, Pasta and Pizza section) but their very rich
  sauces, which often include cheese and sometimes egg.
  A carbonara sauce has the highest calorific value.

Food Category or Brand	Calories /100 g	Portion	Size /g	Calories /port
Chinese				
barbecue spare ribs		each		140
beef in oyster sauce		1 portion		345
butterfly prawns, in batter		1 portion		365
chicken chop suey		1 portion		425
chicken chow mein, noodles		1 portion		715
crab & sweetcorn soup		1 portion		155
egg fu yung		1 portion		745
fried rice		1 portion		555
king prawns in batter		each		185
prawn chop suey		1 portion		310

Food Category or Brand	Calories /100 g	Portion	Size /g	Calories /port
prawn crackers		each		15
shredded beef		1 portion		540
sweet & sour pork		1 portion		860
sweet & sour prawns		1 portion		470
Desserts				
apple fritter		each		65
banana fritter		each		55
chow chow		1 portion		275

French

beef bourguignon		1 portion		530
coq au vin		1 portion		650
duck in orange sauce		1 portion		720
escargots		1 portion		300
French onion soup		1 portion		280
mussels in wine sauce		1 portion		380
scallops in cheese sauce		1 portion		350
sole, grilled		1 portion		310
sole Veronique		1 portion		550
steak au poivre		1 portion		490
tournados rossini		1 portion		600
trout, grilled		1 portion		240

Desserts				
bombe		1 portion		180
chocolate gateau		1 portion		400
chocolate mousse		1 portion		260
crêpes Suzette		1 portion		400
pineapple in Kirsch		1 portion		90

Greek

bean soup		1 portion		250
Greek salad		1 portion		180
houmous with pitta		1 portion		460

Food Category or Brand	Calories /100 g	Portion	Size /g	Calories /port
kalamari, deep fried		1 portion		500
kalamari, marinaded		1 portion		200
kebabs		1 portion		320
meatballs		1 portion		580
moussaka		1 portion		665
stifado		1 portion		565
stuffed vine leaves		1 portion		300
taramasalata with pitta		1 portion		450
tzatziki		1 portion		56

Desserts

halva		1 portion		260
layered pastry (filo)		1 portion		360

Indian

chapati		each		140
chicken curry		1 portion		745
chicken korma		1 portion		870
lamb biriyani		1 portion		920
meat madras		1 portion		545
meat vindaloo		1 portion		565
mixed vegetable curry		1 portion		450
naan bread		each		300
onion bhaji, large		each		245
pilau rice		1 portion		470
plain boiled rice		1 portion		310
poppadum		each		75
pork vindaloo		1 portion		595
potato curry		1 portion		515
prawn biriyani		1 portion		855
roghan ghosh		1 portion		720
samosa		each		260
tandoori chicken		1 portion		310
tomato sambal		1 portion		20

Food Category or Brand	Calories /100 g	Portion	Size /g	Calories /port
Desserts				
glub jamen		1 portion		365
kulfi		1 portion		215
mango slices		1 portion		155

Italian

Antipasti

artichokes	379			
calf's liver with sage		1 portion		270
cannelloni		1 portion		500
lasagne		1 portion		650
mixed fish salad		1 portion		365
mixed fried fish		1 portion		1000
mixed vegetables	330			
mushrooms	381			
Parma ham with figs		1 portion		120
Parma ham with melon		1 portion		150
peppers	331			
ravioli		1 portion		510
scampi provençale	—	1 portion		500
spaghetti bolognese		1 portion		720
spaghetti carbonara		1 portion		1020
spaghetti marinara		1 portion		690
spaghetti napoletana		1 portion		630
spaghetti al pesto		1 portion		855
squid		1 portion		300
stacciatelle		1 portion		100
stuffed tomatoes		1 portion		200
sun-dried tomatoes	387			
Desserts				
cassata		1 portion		150
figs		1 portion		60
profiteroles		1 portion		600

Fast Foods

Most of the items in this listing come from the popular international food chains. These organizations practise 'portion control', so the calorie figures should be fairly accurate. If you are visiting a privately-owned fast food outlet, the figures given here should at least provide an indication of the calorie content of individual dishes on offer.

Here are some bits of advice for slimmers:

- hamburger places: if possible choose a hamburger by itself, without bun or French fries, accompanied by a simple salad. Avoid cheeseburgers and be aware that some barbecue sauces contain surprising amounts of sugar.

- chicken restaurants: ask for grilled or roast chicken instead of fried.

- fish and chips: again, ask for a salad rather than chips — and see if grilled fish is available rather than battered-and-fried.

- pizza restaurants: the problem isn't so much the pizza dough (though you'd do better to ask for the thin and crispy type of base) but the toppings. The basic pizza topping is cheese and tomato, of course — let cheese be the only high-calorie element in the total mix. (See also the separate **Rice, Pasta and Pizza** section).

- **Sandwiches** are in their own section.

- Milk shakes can be found in **Drinks** (Non-alcoholic).

Food Category or Brand	Calories /100 g	Portion	Size /g	Calories /port
Burger King				
BK flamer		each		350
BK spicy beanburger		each		515
bacon double cheeseburger		each		475
cheeseburger		each		295
cheeseburger deluxe		each		345
chicken royale		each		415
crispy cod		each		395
double barbecue BLT		each		445
double cheeseburger		each		430
double whopper		each		575
double whopper, cheese		each		830
French fries, small		1 packet		275
French fries, large		1 packet		400
hamburger		each		255
mushroom double Swiss		each		425
onion rings		1 serving		295
Whopper		each		540
Whopper with cheese		each		615
Desserts				
apple pie		each		220
cherry pie		each		235
Drinks				
chocolate milkshake		each		330
Coca-Cola (small)		each		105
Coca-Cola (large)		each		205
Coca-Cola (regular)		each		165
Diet Coke		each		0
Fanta (small)		each		90
Fanta (large)		each		180
Fanta (regular)		each		145
hot chocolate		each		105
milk		each		195

Food Category or Brand	Calories /100 g	Portion	Size /g	Calories /port
orange juice		each		115
Sprite (small)		each		100
Sprite (large)		each		200
Sprite (regular)		each		160
strawberry milkshake		each		315
vanilla milkshake		each		290
white coffee, no sugar		each		20
white tea, no sugar		each		20

Carveries

Starters

avocado with prawns		1 serving		320
melon		1 serving		40
pâté on toast		1 serving		400
prawn cocktail		1 serving		270
tomato soup		1 serving		80
vegetable soup		1 serving		75

Roast Meats

beef, lean	220	1 serving	50	110
beef, lean & fat	320	1 serving	50	160
chicken	170	1 serving	50	85
chicken with skin	240	1 serving	50	120
lamb, lean	220	1 serving	50	110
lamb, lean & fat	300	1 serving	50	150
pork crackling		1 serving		65
pork, lean	160	1 serving	50	80
port, lean & fat	320	1 serving	50	160
turkey	160	1 serving	50	80
turkey with skin	190	1 serving	50	95

Side Orders

apple sauce		2 tbsp		40
bacon roll		each		25

Food Category or Brand	Calories /100 g	Portion	Size /g	Calories /port
gravy	.	2 tbsp		30
horseradish sauce		1 tsp		10
mint sauce		1 tbsp		5
Yorkshire pudding		1 serving		120
Desserts				
cheesecake		1 serving		390
crème caramel		1 serving		200
fresh fruit salad		1 serving		80
fruit pies, all flavours		1 serving		360
ice-cream, all flavours		2 scoops		225
sherry trifle		1 serving		410
sorbet with wafer		2 scoops		100

Fish & Chip Shops

chicken in batter		1 portion		640
chips, average portion		1 portion		560
chips, large portion		1 portion		860
chips, small portion		1 portion		390
cod in batter		1 portion		330
cod roe in batter		1 portion		200
gherkins, large		each		10
haddock in batter		1 portion		340
mushy peas		1 portion		140
plaice in batter		1 portion		650
rockfish in batter		1 portion		650
sausage in batter		1 portion		225
sausage, jumbo		each		250
saveloy		each		230
scampi in batter		1 portion		240
skate in batter		1 portion		460
tartare sauce		1 sachet		30
tomato ketchup		1 sachet		20
vinegar				0

Food Category or Brand	Calories /100 g	Portion	Size /g	Calories /port
Kentucky Fried Chicken				
barbecued beans, large		each		240
barbecue beans, regular		each		85
burger, cheese & bacon		each		515
chicken		1 piece		220
classic burger		each		420
classic burger & cheese		each		460
corn on the cob		each		180
corn salad, large		each		355
corn salad, regular		each		150
fillet burger		each		385
fillet burger & cheese		each		475
fillet burger, cheese & bacon		each		480
French fries, large		each		375
French fries, regular		each		295
Side Orders				
American biscuit		each		335
Desserts				
apple pie		each		250
Little Chef				
Snacks				
BLT sandwich		each		630
chicken open sandwich		each		320
Starters				
chicken soup		1 serving		125
Mexican dipper		1 serving		405
mushroom dipper		1 serving		390
prawn cocktail		1 serving		260
salmon terrine		1 serving		215
tomato soup		1 serving		160

Food Category or Brand	Calories /100 g	Portion	Size /g	Calories /port
Salads				
coleslaw		1 serving		195
prawn salad		1 serving		555
side salad		1 serving		165
Main Dishes				
Big-7 beefburger		each		1070
Big-7 cheeseburger		each		1180
Big choice chicken		1 serving		805
cheese & ham tagliatelle		1 serving		710
chef's grill		1 serving		1355
chicken platter		1 serving		875
chipped potatoes		1 serving		410
fillet of cod		1 serving		705
fillet of haddock		1 serving		1015
gammon steak		1 serving		805
lemon sole fingers		1 serving		1055
liver & bacon grill		1 serving		1185
scampi platter		1 serving		985
steak platter		1 serving		1280
tagliatelle bolognese		1 serving		540
vegetarian tagliatelle		1 serving		495
whole plaice		1 serving		745
Desserts				
cheesecake, all flavours		1 serving		345
chocolate arctic ice		1 serving		440
chocolate fudge cake		1 serving		385
hot choc 'n' ice		1 serving		480
lemon sorbet		1 serving		100
mint arctic ice		1 serving		385
pancakes with icecream		1 serving		365
raspberry arctic ice		1 serving		305
sugar & lemon pancakes		1 serving		280

Food Category or Brand	Calories /100 g	Portion	Size /g	Calories /port
McDonalds				
Big Mac		each		446
McChicken sandwich		each		372
cheeseburger		each		272
chicken McNuggets (6)		1 serving		276
chicken McNuggets (9)		1 serving		415
chicken McNuggets (20)		1 serving		924
filet-o-fish		each		332
French fries (large)		1 serving		472
French fries (medium)		1 serving		335
French fries (regular)		1 serving		236
hamburger		each		223
quarter pounder		each		400
quarter pounder with cheese		each		492
Sauces				
barbecue sauce		each		45
mild mustard sauce		each		61
sweet & sour sauce		each		46
sweet curry sauce		each		51
Desserts				
apple pie		each		229
birthday cake		per cake		1912
donut, chocolate-flavoured		each		336
donut, cinnamon		each		287
donut, plain		each		275
donut, sugared		each		246
Drinks				
chocolate milkshake		each		303
coffee, half cream		each		19
cola (large)		each		231
cola (medium)		each		147
cola (regular)		each		105

Food Category or Brand	Calories /100 g	Portion	Size /g	Calories /port
hot chocolate		each		119
milk		each		165
orange flavour (large)		each		258
orange flavour (medium)		each		164
orange flavour (regular)		each		117
orange juice (medium)		each		102
orange juice (regular)		each		59
root beer (large)		each		231
root beer (medium)		each		147
root beer (regular)		each		105
strawberry milkshake		each		312
tea, skimmed milk		each		4
vanilla milkshake		each		301

Breakfast Menu

bacon & egg McMuffin		each		320
big breakfast		each		504
buttered English muffin		each		155
buttered muffin with preserves		each		228
hash brown		each		100
sausage & egg McMuffin		each		433

Perfect Pizza

Deep Pan, Medium

beefeater		each		990
ham & mushroom		each		940
ham & pineapple		each		970
special		each		1085
spicy hot one		each		1020
tomato & cheese		each		905
vegetarian		each		920

Deep Pan, Large

beefeater		each		1860

Food Category or Brand	Calories /100 g	Portion	Size /g	Calories /port
ham & mushroom		each		1765
ham & pineapple		each		1825
special		each		2060
spicy hot one		each		1925
tomato & cheese		each		1690
vegetarian		each		1725
Thin Crust, Medium				
beefeater		each		770
ham & mushroom		each		720
ham & pineapple		each		755
special		each		870
spicy hot one		each		800
tomato & cheese		each		685
vegetarian		each		705
Thin Crust, Large				
beefeater		each		1445
ham & mushroom		each		1350
ham & pineapple		each		1410
special		each		1645
spicy hot one		each		1505
tomato & cheese		each		1275
vegetarian		each		1310
Pizza Express				
American		each		930
American hot		each		930
capricciosa		each		885
four seasons		each		890
la reine		each		805
margharita		each		760
marinara		each		700
mushroom		each		705
Napoletana		each		810
neptune		each		785

Food Category or Brand	Calories /100 g	Portion	Size /g	Calories /port
Veneziana		each		755
quattro formaggi		each		760
Side Orders				
garlic bread		1 serving		620
ham & eggs, doughballs		1 serving		505
Desserts				
bombe		each		200
cassata		each		160
chocolate cake		each		420
fresh fruit salad		each		80

Pizza Hut

Pan Pizza, Small

sauce & cheese		each		715
seafood supreme		each		875
spicy hot one		each		780
super supreme		each		965
supreme		each		645
vegetarian		each		735

Thin 'n' Crispy, Small

sauce & cheese		each		460
seafood supreme		each		685
spicy hot one		each		725
super supreme		each		760
supreme		each		645
vegetarian		each		620

Pastas

lasagne		1 serving		530
spaghetti bolognese		1 serving		395
tagliatelle supreme		1 serving		685
tagliatelle verdi vegetarian		1 serving		600

Food Category or Brand	Calories /100 g	Portion	Size /g	Calories /port
Salad				
mixed regular salad		1 serving		140
mixed regular salad				
with dressing		1 serving		330
Priazzos				
Florentine		each		1040
Roma		each		990
Verona		each		1000

Pizzaland

Food Category or Brand	Calories /100 g	Portion	Size /g	Calories /port
Deep Pan, 5-inch				
Caribbean		each		400
cheese & tomato		each		360
hot & spicy		each		400
passionara		each		510
seafood		each		415
spicy chicken		each		400
vegetable special		each		375
Deep Pan, 7-inch				
Caribbean		each		700
cheese & tomato		each		620
four seasons		each		775
hot & spicy		each		710
passionara		each		920
seafood		each		730
spicy chicken		each		700
vegetable special		each		650
Deep Pan, 10-inch				
Caribbean		each		1260
cheese & tomato		each		1100
four seasons		each		1400
hot & spicy		each		1275
passionara		each		1610

Food Category or Brand	Calories /100 g	Portion	Size /g	Calories /port
seafood		each		1325
spicy chicken		each		1260
vegetable special		each		1160
Traditional, 7-inch				
Caribbean		each		370
cheese & tomato		each		330
hot & spicy		each		370
passionara		each		485
seafood		each		385
spicy chicken		each		370
vegetable special		each		345
Traditional, 10-inch				
Caribbean		each		650
cheese & tomato		each		570
four seasons		each		720
hot & spicy		each		655
passionara		each		870
seafood		each		680
spicy chicken		each		650
vegetable special		each		600
Wimpy				
chicken in a bun		each		530
fish & chips		1 serving		465
international grill		1 serving		730
Wimpy grill		1 serving		218
Desserts				
chocolate nut sundae		each		230
fruit & nut sundae		each		235
Drinks				
thick shake		each		250
Whippsy		each		222

Fats and Oils

Fats are solid; oils are liquid. In general, oils are high in polyunsaturates and fats have saturated and mono-unsaturated fats. Saturated fats can leave behind fatty deposits in the blood vessels; polyunsaturates, being more liquid, are less likely to do so — therefore polyunsaturates are considered more healthy for you.

All oils have about 900 kcal per 100 g, as do solid fats such as dripping and lard. All ordinary butters are about 740 kcal per 100 g; this is because they naturally contain about 15 per cent water. Concentrated butter and ghee have had some of the water removed.

The various non-butter spreads usually consist of oil that has been hydrogenated and has had water added through various processes which the manufacturers try very hard to keep secret. Some non-butter spreads contain dairy by-products such as whey and dried butter milk. The many 'light' and 'reduced-fat' varieties usually contain large amounts of water, sometimes in excess of 50 per cent; this is one reason why they are mostly unsuitable for cooking.

Margarines may be made either with animal and vegetable fats, or with vegetable fats alone. In general the soft margarines made from vegetable fats are the ones with the highest proportion of polyunsaturates and the lowest levels of cholesterol.

Food Category or Brand	Calories /100 g

Generic Butter, Margarine & Other Solid Fats

blended butter	740
concentrated butter	870
Cornish butter	740
country spread	685
Dutch unsalted butter	740
ghee	911
olive oil	900
pure beef dripping	900
pure lard	900
slightly salted butter	740

Branded Butter, Margarine & Other Solid Fats

Bejam/Iceland
soft spread	596

Dairy Crest
Clover	689
Clover light	396
Willow	718

Delight
extra low-fat spread	228
low-fat spread	386

Flora
extra light sunflower	378

Granose
diet half-fat spread	364
low-salt margarine	750

Food Category or Brand	Calories /100g
plain margarine	750
soya margarine	753

Kraft
Golden Crown	661
Mello, reduced fat	546
special soft spread	643
Vitalite	739
Vitalite reduced fat	546

Krona
gold	646
silver	643
spreadable	553

Olivio
spread	550

Outline
very low-fat spread	268

Safeway
golden low-fat spread	396
low-fat spread	364
meadow dairy spread	671

Sainsbury's
country light	390
dairy-free margarine	740
garlic butter	695
luxury soft margarine	730
margarine for baking	730
olive gold low-fat spread	545
soft margarine	730
soya half-fat spread	360
soya margarine	745
sunflower margarine	735

Food Category or Brand	Calories /100 g
St Ivel	
gold, for cooking	550
gold, lowest	275
gold, standard	389
gold, unsalted	371
Shape sunflower spread	371
St Michael (Marks & Spencer)	
English churn spread	689
golden	710
lite English spread	396
lite low-fat	370
sunflower lite spread	386
sunflower spread	730
Sunglow	389
Stork	
light blend reduced fat	550
Tesco	
golden blend	678
half-fat sunflower spread	382
Vitaquell	
half-calorie low-fat spread	364

Food Category or Brand	Calories /100g
Waitrose	
soft tub margarine	730
sunflower margarine	739
sunflower soft margarine	739
soya soft margarine	735

Generic Oils

blended vegetable oil	900
corn oil	900
grapeseed oil	900
groundnut oil	900
hazelnut oil	900
olive oil	900
olive oil, extra virgin	900
olive oil, light	900
rapeseed oil	900
sesame oil	900
solid vegetable oil	900
soya oil	900
sunflower oil	900
walnut oil	900

Fish

Comparing the calorific value of various types or cuts of fish is not easy, as one 'serving' of some varieties will include the skin and bones, while for those types that can be filleted the whole portion is edible.

Looked at raw, a typical white fish — sole, plaice, halibut — would be 80 per cent water, 18 per cent protein and 1–2 per cent fat — and with no carbohydrate.

The typical raw 'fatty' or 'oily' fish — herring, for example — would be 64 per cent water, 17 per cent protein and 18 per cent fat (the balance is inedible). Depending on the season, some oily fish can contain up to 30 per cent fat.

Shell fish, like white fish, have relatively little fat.

White fish is best for slimming diets, but even the oily fish contain only polyunsaturated fats (unlike the fat found in animal meat) and are also rich in vitamins A and D.

If you're slimming, steaming or poaching fish adds few calories. Plain grilling is next best, then grilling with oil or butter, then deep-frying, and finally pan-frying. If fish are breaded, not only the breadcrumbs but the milk and egg used to bind them will add fats and carbohydrate to the dish.

Many branded products include fish in various sauces or in pies. These additional ingredients must be accounted for, particularly cheese or butter sauces, which will add calories in the form of fat.

Smoked or other forms of cured fish will contain less water, which means that, weight for weight, all nutrients will be more concentrated.

Fish can be canned in brine, tomato or oil — brine adds

least to overall calorific value, tomato sauce most, oil somewhere in between.

The effects of marinating fish will depend on what's in the marinade — some contain sugars.

Food Category or Brand	Calories /100 g	Portion	Size /g	Calories /port
Generic Fish				
abalone canned	146	1 serving	120	175
anchovies canned	143	1 serving	85	122
per fillet		1 fish		5
bass steamed	127	1 serving	85	108
steamed (with bone)	67	1 serving	120	80
bloaters grilled	255	1 serving	50	128
grilled (skin & bones)	189	1 serving	85	161
bream red, steamed	118	1 serving	85	100
steamed (with bones)	61	1 serving	120	73
sea, steamed (bones)	66	1 serving	120	79
brill steamed	115	1 serving	85	100
buckling fillets	214	1 serving	120	257
catfish fried	200	1 serving	85	170
fried (with bone)	188	1 serving	120	225
steamed (with bone)	100	1 serving	120	120
clams fresh, without shell	89	1 serving	120	107
cockles fresh	48	1 serving	85	40
cod fried	139	1 serving	85	120
fried in batter	203	1 serving	85	195
grilled	160	1 serving	85	135
grilled (skin & bones)	136	1 serving	100	135
steamed	82	1 serving	85	70
steamed (skin & bones)	66	1 serving	120	80
cod roe baked in vinegar	128	1 serving	85	110
fried	206	1 serving	85	175
conger fried (with bones)	252	1 serving	100	255
steamed	110	1 serving	85	95
steamed (skin & bones)	83	1 serving	100	85

Food Category or Brand	Calories /100 g	Portion	Size /g	Calories /port
crab boiled	127	1 serving	85	105
boiled (with shell)	25	1 crab	105	
dabs fried (with bones)	199	1 serving	85	170
dogfish fried (with bones)	300	1 serving	85	255
eels silver, stewed	374	1 serving	85	320
fish cakes fried	171	2 cakes	85	145
fishfingers fried	175	5 fingers	85	150
fish paste	174	spread	10	20
flounder fried (with bones)	147	1 serving	120	175
steamed	95	1 serving	85	80
steamed (skin & bones)	53	1 serving	120	65
gurnet grey, steamed (skin & bones)	108	1 serving	120	130
red, steamed (skin & bones)	93	1 serving	120	110
haddock fresh, fried (skin & bone)	161	1 serving	120	190
fresh, steamed	97	1 serving	85	80
fresh, steamed (skin & bone)	74	1 serving	120	90
smoked, steamed	65	1 serving	120	80
hake steamed (skin & bones)	86	1 serving	120	105
halibut steamed	130	1 serving	85	110
steamed (skin & bones)	99	1 serving	120	120
herring baked (with bones)	174	1 serving	100	175
fried	235	1 serving	85	200
fried (with bones)	208	1 serving	100	210
herring roe fried	260	1 serving	85	220
john dory steamed (skin & bones)	59	1 serving	100	60
kippers baked	201	1 serving	85	170
baked (skin & bones)	108	1 serving	100	110
lemon sole fried (skin & bones)	173	1 serving	100	175
steamed	90	1 serving	85	75
steamed (skin & bones)	64	1 serving	100	65

Food Category or Brand	Calories /100 g	Portion	Size /g	Calories /port
ling fried (skin & bones)	186	1 serving	100	175
lobster boiled	119	1 serving	85	100
mackerel fried (skin & bones)	136	1 serving	100	135
monkfish fried (with bones)	145	1 serving	100	145
steamed (with bones)	79	1 serving	100	80
mullet grey, steamed (skin & bones)	81	1 serving	120	100
red, steamed (with bones)	85	1 serving	120	100
mussels boiled	87	1 serving	85	75
boiled (with shells)	26	1 serving	85	25
oysters raw	50	1 serving	85	43
pilchards canned	220	1 serving	85	185
plaice fried (with bones)	142	1 serving	100	140
steamed	92	1 serving	85	75
steamed (skin & bones)	50	1 serving	100	50
prawns cooked	104	1 serving	85	90
cooked (with shells)	40	1 serving	150	60
saithe steamed	98	1 serving	85	85
steamed (with bones)	83	1 serving	100	85
salmon canned (with liquid)	137	1 serving	85	115
fresh, steamed	199	1 serving	85	170
fresh, steamed (skin & bones)	161	1 serving	100	160
smoked	175	1 serving	85	150
sardines canned, oil	222	1 serving	50	150
canned, tomato	179	1 serving	50	90
scallops steamed	105	1 serving	85	90
shrimps cooked	114	1 serving	85	95
cooked (with shells)	38	1 serving	150	57
skate fried (with bones)	201	1 serving	85	170
smelts fried	408	1 serving	85	345
sole fried	274	1 serving	85	230
fried (with bones)	241	1 serving	120	290
steamed	84	1 serving	85	70

Food Category or Brand	Calories /100 g	Portion	Size /g	Calories /port
steamed (skin & bones)	50	1 serving	120	60
sprats bones & head, fresh,				
fried	390	1 serving	120	465
smoked, grilled	284	1 serving	120	340
sturgeon steamed (with bones)	105	1 serving	120	125
trout steamed (skin & bones)	88	1 serving	120	105
sea, steamed (skin & bones)	104	1 serving	120	125
tuna canned (in oil)	1300	1 serving	85	1105
canned, solids only	757	1 serving	85	645
turbot steamed	100	1 serving	85	85
steamed (skin & bone)	66	1 serving	120	80
whelks fresh	91	1 serving	85	80
with shells		each		14
whitebait fried	537	1 serving	50	270
whiting fried (skin & bones)	174	1 serving	120	210
steamed (skin & bones)	61	1 serving	120	75
winkles boiled	75	1 serving	120	90
boiled (with shell)		each		14

Branded Canned Fish

John West

cod roe, soft	85
crab, white meat	53
herring fillets, savoury	168
herring fillets, tomato	190
kipper fillets, drained	163
mackerel fillets, oil	164
mackerel fillets, tomato	140
mackerel, peppered	290
mackerel, smoked, drained	218
mussels, smoked	186
oysters, smoked	195
pilchards, brine	123

Food Category or Brand	Calories /100 g	Portion	Size /g	Calories /port
pilchards, tomato	132			
prawns, drained	60			
salmon, pink	157			
salmon, red	167			
sardines, brine	146			
sardines, oil	158			
sardines, tomato	217			
shrimp, drained	60			
sild, oil	145			
sild, tomato	241			
skippers, oil	180			
tuna, barbecue sauce	151			
tuna, brine	85			
tuna, oil	123			
tuna, tomato	111			
Princes				
anchovy fillets, oil	150			
cockles in vinegar	50			
crab, brine	55			
crab, dressed	128			
herring, marinaded	134			
tuna chunks, brine	79			
tuna chunks, oil	147			
tuna flakes, brine	70			
tuna flakes, mayonnaise	175			
tuna flakes, oil	165			
tuna steaks, brine	75			

Branded Frozen/Chilled Fish

Bejam/Iceland

cod bake		1 serving		297
cod bites		each		34
cod crumble		1 serving		485

Food Category or Brand	Calories /100 g	Portion	Size /g	Calories /port
cod fillets, supercrumb	296			
cod & prawn pie		1 serving		408
cod steaks, breaded		each		111
haddock en croute		1 serving		343
haddock steaks, breaded		each		111
plaice fillets, supercrumb	257			
scampi, breaded	321			
Birds Eye				
Captain's Quarter Pounder		1 serving		245
cod fish finger		1 serving		50
cod fish finger, wholemeal		1 serving		50
cod steak in butter sauce		1 serving		160
cod steak in cheese sauce		1 serving		170
Cod Steak in Crunch Crumbs		1 serving		220
cod steak in parsley sauce		1 serving		155
cod steak, Waferlight Batter		1 serving		195
Fish Feast with cheese		1 serving		220
haddock fish finger		1 serving		50
kipper fillets, buttered	222			
Oven-Crispy Cod		1 serving		230
Prime Fish Cake		1 serving		115
Prime Fish in parsley sauce		1 serving		135
in cheese & tomato sauce		1 serving		190
salmon fish cake		1 serving		90
smoked haddock	99			
Trad. Crispy Haddock Steak		1 serving		225
Value Fish Cake		1 serving		85
Sainsbury's				
4 fish cakes		each		120
cod in butter sauce		1 packet	170	185
cod fillet, mornay sauce		1 packet	284	345
cod medallions	215	1 packet	200	
cod nuggets	215	1 packet	200	

Food Category or Brand	Calories /100 g	Portion	Size /g	Calories /port
cod in parsley sauce		1 packet	170	155
crab pâté	220			
fish crumble		1 packet	284	360
mariners pie		each	227	225
seafarer's pie		each	454	430
smoked mackerel pâté	445			
tuna pâté	290			

St Michael (Marks & Spencer)

cod & seafood toppers	176			
cod bites	200			
filled plaice mornay	94			
fish fricasse	103			
haddock & cheese toppers	254			
haddock steaks in 'lower fat' ovencrisp crumb	145			
haddock steams in ovencrisp batter	192			
layered cod & potato snack	210			
lemon sole in freshbake crumb	221			
plaice goujons with tartare sauce	264			
poached salmon terrine	329			
prawns in cream sauce	142			
salmon en croûte	292			
salmon paupiettes	165			
smoked mackerel pâté	384			
whole scampi in light & crispy crumbs	259			

Waitrose

decorated salmon steaks	158			
layered fish terrine	216			
prawn brioche	248			
salmon en croute	249			

Food Category or Brand	Calories /100 g	Portion	Size /g	Calories /port
smoked mackerel pâté	338			
smoked salmon parcels	140			
smoked salmon pâté	258			
smoked salmon roulade	322			
smoked salmon terrine	157			
Young's				
cod & parsley croquettes	192			
cod & prawn pies	195			
fish kebabs, fresh	56			
fish kebabs, smoked	134			
fresh cod fishcakes	213			
garlic prawns	75			
lemon sole fillets	82			
oriental prawns	110			
sea scallops	93			
smoked haddock fillets	87			
trout amande	160			

Fruit

Fresh fruit is between 80 and 90 per cent water. Most of the energy fruit provides is in the form of sugar — glucose, fructose (a form of sugar peculiar to fruit) and sucrose. Bananas and grapes have, among the fruits commonly available, the highest proportion of sugars.

The actual amount of sugar in any fruit depends on when it was picked. Most fruits do not contain significant amounts of fat, though there are some notable exceptions — olives, with up to 20 per cent for some varieties, and avocados, which are usually also around 15 to 20 per cent but can be as much as 40 per cent.

Fruit oils are, of course, polyunsaturated.

Although this book is only about the calorific values of foods, it's worth mentioning that fruit is, of course, an extremely good source of vitamin C.

Stewing is the most common method of cooking fruit. As a rough guide, the effect of adding a normal amount of sugar to the water used for stewing is to multiply by 2½–3 the calorific value of a portion: apples stewed without sugar end up at 25 kcal/100 g; with added sugar in stewing they are 74 kcal/100 g.

In a dried fruit, such as apricots, the water constituent drops from around 85 per cent down to 25 per cent; all the other values obviously increase in proportion. By the time they are reconstituted, the water proportion is back to about 65 per cent. Many people would add sugar when they reconstitute: if no sugar is added, a 100g portion would contain about 85 calories; once sugar is added, the portion contains 120 to 125 calories.

Most canned fruit is sunk into syrup rather than juice. This added syrup usually at least doubles the calorific value per portion.

Crystallized fruit is made by dipping fruit into a hot sugar solution. If you are slimming, avoid at all costs!

Food Category or Brand	Calories /100 g	Portion	Size /g	Calories /port
Generic Fruits				
Apples				
cooking, baked (flesh only)	39	1 serving	130	50
cooking, baked (with skin)	31	1 serving	150	45
cooking, raw	37	1 apple	200	75
cooking, stewed (no sugar)	28	1 serving	150	45
eating (flesh only)	47	1 serving	130	60
eating (skin & core)	35	1 apple	185	65
Apricots				
canned, in syrup	106	1 serving	85	90
dried, no soak	125			
dried, stewed (no sugar)	61	1 serving	85	50
fresh	28	3 fruit	95	30
fresh (with stone)	26	3 fruit	120	30
fresh, stewed (no sugar)	22	1 serving	100	20
Babaco				
flesh only	43	1 serving	130	
whole fruit, no seeds		1 fruit		195
Bananas				
fresh	77	1 banana		100
with skin	45	1 banana		100
Bilberries				
raw & frozen	57	1 serving	100	

Food Category or Brand	Calories /100 g	Portion	Size /g	Calories /port
Blackberries				
raw	30	1 serving	100	30
stewed (no sugar)	23	1 serving	100	23
Blackcurrants				
canned, in syrup	82	1 serving	100	82
raw & frozen	28	1 serving	100	28
stewed, no sugar	25	1 serving	100	25
Blueberries				
raw & frozen	64	1 serving	100	64
Cherries				
cooking, raw (with stones)	39	1 serving	100	39
raw (with stones)	40	1 serving	100	40
stewed (without sugar)	35	1 serving	100	35
Cranberries				
jelly	143	1 tbsp		25
raw	14	1 serving	100	
sauce	15	½ cup		200
Currants				
black, raw	29			
black, stewed (no sugar)	22			
dried	244			
red, raw	21			
red, stewed (no sugar)	16			
white, raw	26			
white, stewed (no sugar)	20			
Damsons				
raw (with stones)	34	1 serving	100	34
stewed, no sugar (stones)	29	1 serving	100	29
Dates				
dried	272			
fresh	248	1 serving	100	248
fresh, with stones	214	1 serving	120	255

Food Category or Brand	Calories /100 g	Portion	Size /g	Calories /port
Figs				
dried, raw	214	1 serving	50	110
dried, stewed (no sugar)	107	1 serving	100	110
green	41	1 serving	100	40
Fruit Salad				
canned, in syrup	94	1 serving	120	110
Ginger Stem				
canned, in syrup	214	1 serving	120	257
Gooseberries				
green, raw	17			
ripe	37	1 serving	120	45
stewed (no sugar)	13	1 serving	120	15
Grapefruit				
fresh	22	½ grapefruit		45
with skin & pips	11	½ grapefruit		23
Grapes				
black (skin, pips & stalks)	51	1 serving	150	75
white (skin, pips & stalks)	60	1 serving	150	90
Greengages				
fresh, with stones	45	1 serving	120	55
stewed, no sugar (stones)	37	1 serving	120	45
Guava				
canned	61	1 serving	85	52
fresh	57	1 serving	120	68
Kiwi				
fresh	107			
Kumquat				
fresh	64	1 serving	120	
whole fruit		1 fruit		5

Food Category or Brand	Calories /100 g	Portion	Size /g	Calories /port
Lemons				
juice	7	glass	100	5
whole fruit	15	1 fruit	100	15
Loganberries				
canned, in syrup	101	1 serving	110	100
fresh	17	1 serving	120	20
stewed (no sugar)	13	1 serving	120	15
Lychee				
canned	68	1 serving	110	74
fresh	28	1 fruit	50	14
Mandarins				
canned	64	glass	100	65
fresh (with skin)	45	1 mandarin		50
Mango				
raw, flesh only	61	1 serving	120	73
Mangosteen				
whole fruit	71	1 fruit	65	20
Medlars				
flesh	43	1 serving	120	52
Melons				
cantaloupe (flesh)	24	½ melon	130	55
cantaloupe (with skin)	15	½ melon	360	55
charentais (flesh)	11	½ melon	300	33
honeydew	13	½ melon	300	39
ogen	15	½ melon	300	45
water (flesh)	54	wedge	300	162
yellow (with skin)	13	½ melon	300	40
Mulberries				
fresh	36			

Food Category or Brand	Calories /100 g	Portion	Size /g	Calories /port
Nectarines				
fresh (with stones)	46	1 serving	120	55
Olives				
with stones	85	1 serving	85	70
Oranges				
fresh	35	1 orange	140	50
fresh, with peel & pips	27	1 orange	185	50
juice, canned	217			
juice, from concentrate	157			
juice, fresh	38	glass	150	55
juice, frozen				
juice, frozen, diluted	45	glass	150	65
Ortaniques				
flesh	57			
flesh with skin	43			
whole fruit		1 fruit	142	60
Passion fruit				
with skin	15			
Papaw (Papaya)				
fresh, flesh only	39	1 serving	110	43
Peaches				
canned, in syrup	87	1 serving	100	87
dried, raw	213			
dried, stewed (no sugar)	70	1 serving	100	70
fresh	37	1 peach	110	40
fresh (with stones)	32	1 peach	125	40
Pears				
canned, in syrup	77	1 serving	120	90
cooking, raw (fresh)	36			
cooking, stewed (no sugar)	27	1 serving	120	35
eating, fresh	40	1 pear	175	70
eating, flesh (incl. core)	30	1 pear	250	70

Food Category or Brand	Calories /100 g	Portion	Size /g	Calories /port
Pineapple				
canned, in syrup	77	1 serving	100	77
fresh	46	1 serving	100	46
Plums				
cooking, raw, fresh (skins)	26			
cooking, raw (with stones)	23	1 serving	120	25
dessert, raw	38	1 plum		20
dessert, raw (stones)	36	1 plum		20
stewed, no sugar (stones)	20	1 serving	120	25
Pomegranate				
juice	44	glass	100	44
Prunes				
dried, raw, pitted	161			
dried, raw (with stones)	134			
stewed, no sugar (stones)	81	1 serving	100	81
Quinces				
fresh	25			
Raisins				
dried	247			
Raspberries				
raw	25	1 serving	120	30
stewed (no sugar)	23	1 serving	100	23
Rhubarb				
stewed (no sugar)	5	1 serving	120	10
Sharon Fruit				
fresh	78	1 serving	100	
whole fruit		1 fruit		130
Strawberries				
fresh (no stalk)	26	1 serving	120	30

Food Category or Brand	Calories /100 g	Portion	Size /g	Calories /port
Sultanas				
dried	249			
Tangerines				
fresh	34	1 tangerine	120	40
with peel & pips	24	1 tangerine	120	30
Topaz				
flesh only	57	1 serving	120	
flesh & skin	39	1 serving	120	
whole fruit		1 fruit		65
Ugli Fruit				
flesh only	53	1 serving	120	
flesh & skin	36	1 serving	120	
whole fruit		1 fruit		140

Ice-cream

Commercial ice-creams are made from milk, cream, milk products, non-milk fats, flavourings, stabilizers and emulsifiers. The other big ingredient is sugar.

'Dairy' ice-creams must contain at least 5 per cent milk fat and must not contain any other sort of fat (except that found in egg yolk). The luxury dairy ice-creams often contain 15 or more per cent milk fat/cream. In 'non-dairy' ice-creams, other fats, such as vegetable oils may be used.

All ice-cream contains air as part of its structure — soft ice-cream contains more air than traditional types. In a traditional dairy ice-cream, half of its volume is air.

Water accounts for about 60 to 70 per cent of an ice-cream's weight, protein about 4 per cent, fat about 10 per cent (mostly saturated and monounsaturated) and carbohydrate (nearly all sugar) just under 25 per cent. Some flavoured ice-creams have considerably more sugar.

A sorbet or water ice will usually have, weight for weight, half the calories of a dairy ice. There's no milk, cream or other oil, of course — but there *is* plenty of sugar.

Mousses appear in the **Desserts** section.

A serving is 100 g, unless stated otherwise.

Food Category or Brand	Calories /100 g	Portion	Size /g	Calories /port
Branded Ice-creams				
Bejam/Iceland				
black cherry & Kirsch	169			
cassata	165			
chocolate 'n' nut	225			
chocolate orange (Cointreau)	169			
crunchy toffee	201			
ice-cream roll		⅙ roll		82
mint chocolate chip	169			
neapolitan	165			
neapolitan chequers	162			
passion fruit & peach	179			
raspberry ripple	169			
strawberry vanilla bombe		whole		193
vanilla (economy)	123			
white vanilla	158			
CHOC ICES				
chocolate 'n' nut		1 choc ice		119
dark mint		1 choc ice		115
chocolate 'n' nut cornet		1 cornet		258
chocolate 'n' nut sundae		1 sundae		177
Bertorelli				
cassata bombe dairy	215	1 bombe		614
chocolate dairy	211			
chocolate menthe	233			
coffee	196			
lemon surprise	225			
lemon water ice	109			
mela menthe	306	each		213
mela parisienne	302	each		211
mela stragata	298	each		208
orange surprise	220			

Food Category or Brand	Calories /100 g	Portion	Size /g	Calories /port
orange water ice	110			
praline dairy	210			
raspberry water ice	101			
strawberry dairy	176			
vanilla dairy	202			
Haagan-Dazs				
choc choc chip	244			
macadamia nut brittle	243			
praline & cream	248			
strawberry	210			
vanilla	230			
Loseley				
acacia honey & ginger	188			
apricot sorbet	79			
blackcurrant sorbet	69			
Brazilian mocha	212			
lemon sorbet	67			
Montezuma chocolate	167			
passion fruit	66			
pineapple sorbet	74			
sovereign strawberry	160			
vanilla, old-fashioned	202			
woodland hazel	200			
Lyons Maid				
COCKTAIL				
Blue Hawaiian		each		34
Brandy Alexander		each		81
Piña Colada		each		60
CUTTING BRICKS				
chocolate ripple	181			
neapolitan	179			
peach Melba	177			

Food Category or Brand	Calories /100 g	Portion	Size /g	Calories /port
raspberry ripple	173			
vanilla	182			
GOLD SEAL				
caramel toffee	210			
chocolate coconut flake	183			
chocolate swirl	192			
mint chocolate chip	196			
rum & raisin	184			
vanilla chocolate flake	219			
Ross				
chocolate	180			
chocolate ripple	180			
Cornish dairy	160			
raspberry ripple	170			
strawberry	170			
vanilla	170			
vanilla choc ices	290	1 choc ice		130
Safeway				
banana, soft scoop	169			
chocolate, soft scoop	167			
Cornish vanilla brick	169			
economy ice-cream	179			
ice-cream roll	178			
LUXURY				
apple pie	228			
country strawberry	218			
egg nog & raisin	229			
Georgia pecan pie	239			
Jaffa orange	221			
maple & walnut	233			
mocha almond	259			
orange ice lollies	42			

Food Category or Brand	Calories /100 g	Portion	Size /g	Calories /port
Piña Colada dairy	221			
praline & toffee dairy	230			
raspberry ripple, brick	164			
raspberry ripple, soft	172			
strawberry brick	182			
tin roof dairy	242			
vanilla brick	182			
vanilla choc ices	263			
vanilla dairy	225			
vanilla, soft scoop	169			
Sainsbury's				
blackcurrant fruit dairy	190			
chocolate ribonette dairy	190			
strawberry, natural	190			
vanilla	190			
vanilla, natural	190			
St Michael (Marks & Spencer)				
orange juice bars	90			
raspberry ripple dairy	174			
rum & raisin	200			
vanilla dairy	178			
vanilla, luxury dairy	265			
vanilla, soft scoop	183			
walnut supreme	239			
Waitrose				
blackcurrant sorbet	132			
chocolate	185			
coffee	154			
Cornish dairy	173			
lemon sorbet	114			
passion fruit sorbet	125			
raspberry ripple	193			
vanilla, soft	155			

Food Category or Brand	Calories /100 g	Portion	Size /g	Calories /port
AMERICAN STYLE				
chocolate chip	194			
chocolate orange	195			
mint chocolate chip	199			
strawberry & cream	178			
CHOC ICES				
chocolate chip	309			
dark	290			
milk	290			
pineapple & coconut	288			

Wall's

ALPINE				
chocolate	209			
orange sorbet	142			
strawberry	200			
vanilla	209			
BRICKS				
bananarama	158			
Cornish vanilla	183			
cream of Cornish	183			
golden vanilla	176			
neapolitan	176			
Piña Colada	148			
raspberry ripple	176			
rum & raisin	183			
strawberry ripple	183			
CARTE D'OR				
cherry Kirsch	121			
chocolate	126			
coffee	115			
lemon sorbet	130			
strawberry	120			

Food Category or Brand	Calories /100 g	Portion	Size /g	Calories /port
vanilla	123			
walnut	138			
CORNETTO				
chocolate 'n' nut		each		205
neapolitan		each		195
strawberry		each		190
tutti frutti		each		230
INDIVIDUAL				
Chunky Choc	204	each		165
Dairy Milk ice cream	291	each		196
Feast		each		260
Magnum	239	each		289
Magnum White	242	each		293
Mini Fruit		each		30
Mini Milk, strawberry		each		40
Mini Milk, vanilla		each		85
Pineapple Split		each		85
Strawberry Split		each		80
Tongue Twister		each		85
ITALIANO				
chocolate & nut Capri	211			
fruits of the forest	158			
mint chocolate croccante	229			
strawberry Rosama	158			
toffee fudge Caramella	201			
Tutti Frutti Classico	183			
SOFT SCOOP				
Blue Ribbon vanilla	176			
golden vanilla	183			
raspberry ripple	176			
rum & raisin	183			

Food Category or Brand	Calories /100 g	Portion	Size /g	Calories /port
SPECIALS				
Cassata Denise log		whole		585
Mint Whip		whole		200
Viennetta		whole		815
TOO GOOD TO BE TRUE				
chocolate	88			
double toffee	89			
peanut choc	91			
TWINPACK				
bananarama	158			
Hawaiian Punch	165			
strawberry & chocolate	183			
strawberry & vanilla	176			
summer days	158			
Weight Watchers				
Neopolitan	93	serving		68
vanilla	96	serving		69

Jams, Spreads, Sauces and Pickles

A true jam, made properly with sugar as a preservative, is usually about 250 kcal per 100 g; 70 g of that will be carbohydrate in the form of sugar. In a reduced-sugar formula, the carbohydrate content may be only 30 to 35 g out of the total 100 and the calorific value will be down to around 125.

The really high-calorie spreads are the nut spreads (except for peanut butter), particularly those that also contain chocolate. A hazelnut chocolate spread can contain, weight for weight, more than twice the calories of a regular fruit jam.

Butter is listed in the **Fats and Oils** section; pâtés can be found in the sections on **Fish** and **Meat and Poultry**; cheese spreads are in the **Dairy Products** section.

The calorific value of pickles usually depends on the amount of sugar used in the pickling brine.

Food Category or Brand	Calories /100 g	Portion	Size /g	Calories /port

Branded Jams and Spreads

Boots

honey	288			
peanut butter	605			
savoury spread	205			

Food Category or Brand	Calories /100 g	Portion	Size /g	Calories /port
Cadbury's				
chocolate spread	315			
hazelnut chocolate spread	570			
Chivers				
lemon curd	285			
marmalade, all types	255			
Crosse & Blackwell				
redcurrant jelly	259			
Ferrero				
Nutella	525			
Gales				
honey, all types	310			
lemon curd	280			
peanut butter	586			
Granose Sandwich Spreads				
cereals	225			
herbs	265			
mushrooms	337			
olives	308			
soya bean paste	140			
tastex	208			
vegetable pâté	296			
Hartley's				
jelly jams	260			
lemon cheese	295			
marmalade	255			
mincemeat	285			
pure fruit jams	255			
Heinz				
celery, corn & apple	188			
cucumber sandwich	183			

Food Category or Brand	Calories /100 g	Portion	Size /g	Calories /port
Marmite				
		1 teasp.		13
Moorhouse				
jams, all flavours	255			
lemon cheese	295			
lemon curd	285			
marmalade	250			
mincemeat	285			
Prewetts				
honey & sesame spread	439			
mincemeat	287			
peanut butter	596			
Princes Pastes				
beef	212			
chicken & ham	203			
crab	139			
ham & beef	139			
salmon	103			
sardine & tomato	152			
Robertson's				
jams, all flavours	251			
lemon curd	291			
marmalade, all types	251			
mincemeat, all flavours	266			
pure fruit spreads, all flavours	120			
Rose's				
marmalade, all types	255			
Safeway				
beef paste	225			
chicken & ham paste	225			
crab paste	186			
hazelnut spread	586			

Food Category or Brand	Calories /100 g	Portion	Size /g	Calories /port
honey, all types	291			
jams, all flavours	253			
lemon curd	290			
marmalade, all types	252			
mincemeat, all flavours	269			
no-added-sugar jams	140			
salmon & shrimp paste	183			
savoury spread	224			
St Michael (Marks & Spencer)				
ham spread	193			
honey, all types	290			
jams, all flavours	240			
potted beef	170			
potted crab, butter	180			
potted salmon, butter	166			
tuna spread, mayonnaise	329			
Spar				
conserves, all types	247			
Sun-Pat				
hazelnut chocolate spread	526			
peanut butter	174			
wholenut peanut butter	175			
Waitrose				
fruit spreads, all flavours	124			
hazelnut spread	530			
honey, all types	304			
jams, all flavours	248			
lemon cheese	329			
lemon curd	276			
marmalade, all types	248			
mincemeat	275			
peanut butter	600			

Food Category or Brand	Calories /100 g	Portion	Size /g	Calories /port
reduced-sugar jams, all flavs.	124			
stem ginger in syrup	260			

Generic Sauces & Pickles
mayonnaise (low-calorie)	350			
mayonnaise (regular)	725			

Branded Sauces & Pickles

Coleman's
MUSTARDS

American	110			
Dijon	170			
French	115			
German	135			
horseradish	140			
mild burger	110			
wholegrain	145			

CONDIMENTS

apple sauce	80			
cranberry & wine sauce	215			
creamed horseradish	200			
mint jelly	265			
prawn cocktail sauce	380			

Sainsbury's
barbecue relish	125			
beetroot pickle	65			
burger relish	175			
cider vinegar	2			
cocktail cherries	175			
corn relish	140			
courgette chutney	95			

Food Category or Brand	Calories /100 g	Portion	Size /g	Calories /port
cucumber relish	135			
curried fruit chutney	145			
Dijon mustard	145			
dill cucumbers	25			
English mustard	180			
malt vinegar	6			
midget gherkins	5			
mild mustard relish	130			
mustard with herbs	100			
piccalilli	50			
pickled onions	25			
pickled red cabbage	15			
pitted black olives	195			
pitted green olives	210			
red wine vinegar	4			
sauerkraut	25			
silverskin onions	13			
sweet onions	15			
sweet piccalilli	105			
tomato & chilli relish	130			
tomato relish	125			
white wine vinegar	3			
whole baby beets	45			

Waitrose

apple & onion chutney	57			
apple chutney	55			
apricot chutney	52			
bolognese sauce	17			
carbonara	58			
cheese sauce	54			
cocktail gherkins	9			
cocktail onions	16			
creamed horseradish	103			
curry chutney	60			

Food Category or Brand	Calories /100 g	Portion	Size /g	Calories /port
fruit sauce	44			
garlic mayonnaise	294			
lemon mayonnaise	294			
low-calorie vinegar & oil				
dressing	54			
mango chutney	72			
mayonnaise	294			
mint sauce	65			
mustard piccalilli				
napoletana	9			
peach chutney	61			
reduced-calorie mayonnaise	114			
salad cream	112			
seafood dressing	180			
spicy sauce	31			
squeezed tomato ketchup	18			
sweet baby beetroot	6			
tartar sauce	157			
tomato chutney	57			
tomato ketchup	33			
tzatziki	83			

Meat and Poultry

Meat

Some cuts of meat include bone, skin, gristle and other inedible elements, so computing their exact calorific content can be a bit difficult.

Beef (without bone) will be about two-thirds water, 18 to 24 per cent protein and 10 to 20 per cent fat. The visible fat is mostly saturated, but all meats have veins of fat running through the flesh as well. The amount of visible fat may vary from 50 to 60 per cent (in the case of streaky bacon) down to below 20 per cent for so-called 'lean' meats. A great deal of the flavour of meat comes from the fat.

In general terms there is very little nutritional difference between various cuts from the same animal – the more expensive ones will be the most tender, while the cheaper ones will require slow cooking over a low heat or marinating to soften the tissues up. Of course, certain portions come with more fat attached, but this is partly a function of how the butcher has divided the cuts.

Pork is the fattiest meat commonly eaten, followed by lamb and then beef.

As far as cooking methods are concerned, the following would be the order of preference for someone who wants to minimize his or her fat intake: grilling (without basting), roasting (again without too much basting or using additional fats), boiling, simmering, stewing (where the cooking liquid is retained as part of the dish), frying. There are of course exceptions: oxtail is stewed and the liquid retained, but most cooks would skim the fat from the liquid before serving.

The weight of some frozen meat joints, particularly bacon and its relatives, is sometimes artificially boosted with additional water. The weights given here for frozen meat do not include this additional water.

Sausages, salamis and the like can be found in the **Processed Meats** section.

Poultry

The calorific value of poultry also depends largely on how much fat is on the meat. We can compare poultry that has been roasted: roast turkey is between 2 and 3 per cent fat, roast chicken between 5 and 6 per cent fat, roast grouse 5 per cent, partridge 7 per cent, pheasant 9 per cent, duck 10 per cent fat, pigeon 13 per cent and goose 22 per cent. Most of the fats found in poultry are monounsaturated and saturated. The remainder of the energy in poultry comes from meat proteins.

Fats add to the flavour of poultry and, especially in the case of turkey, the lack of fat can sometimes result in meat that is unacceptably dry – which is why most people lay strips of bacon over their turkey when they roast it.

The weight of some frozen poultry is artificially boosted by the injection of additional water.

The low-fat cooking methods are boiling (with the fluid discarded), grilling and barbecuing, tandoor cooking, roasting (with minimal basting and no additional fats) and stewing. Frying will inevitably add both carbohydrates and fat – the breadcrumbs provide the carbohydrates, the binder provides fat, and of course the cooking fat gets absorbed as well.

Increasingly, chicken and turkey are being offered in manufactured forms, such as pre-prepared roasts, or cuts cooked in Italian, Chinese or Indian style. You can also get shaped and breaded escalopes, frozen 'boneless joints' (in which turkey meat is surrounded with a layer of pork fat), and a number of derivatives of chicken kiev in which a pocket of meat is filled with butter and garlic (the classic kiev recipe) or various sauce/cheese/vegetable combinations. Inevitably the butter and cheese increase the fat — and cholesterol. See the Ready-made Meals section.

Look in the **Fast Foods** section for information about fried chicken take-away.

Food Category or Brand	Calories /100 g	Portion	Size /g	Calories /port
Generic Meat				
Beef				
corned beef	231	1 slice	30	75
silverside, boiled	301	1 serving	85	190
sirloin, roast, lean	224	1 serving	85	190
sirloin, roast, lean & fat	385	1 serving	85	325
steak, fried	273	1 serving	85	230
steak, grilled	304	1 serving	85	260
steak, stewed	206	1 serving	85	175
topside, boiled	213	1 serving	85	180
topside, roast, lean	249	1 serving	85	210
topside, roast, lean & fat	321	1 serving	85	270
Veal				
calf's brain, boiled	103	1 serving	100	103
calf's liver, fried	262	1 serving	85	220
cutlet, fried	215	1 serving	85	185
fillet, roast	231	1 serving	85	195
Brawn	153	1 serving	120	
Hare				
roast	193	1 serving	85	165
roast, with bone	131	1 serving	100	131
stewed	194	1 serving	85	165

Food Category or Brand	Calories /100 g	Portion	Size /g	Calories /port
stewed, with bone	142	1 serving	100	142

Also see **Rabbit**

Luncheon Meats
canned	335	1 serving	85	295
meat paste	173	spread	20	35

Mutton
chop, grilled, lean	271	1 serving	90	240
chop, grilled, lean without bone	127	1 serving	120	150
chop, grilled, lean & fat without bone	378	1 serving	120	450
chop, fried, lean & fat without bone	512	1 serving	120	615
leg, boiled	260	1 serving	100	260
leg, roast	292	1 serving	100	326
scrag & neck, stewed	326	1 serving	100	326
scrag & neck, stewed without bone	245	1 serving	120	295
sheep's brain, boiled	110	1 serving	100	110
sheep's heart, roast	239	1 serving	85	205
sheep's kidney, fried	199	1 serving	85	170
sheep's tongue, stewed	296	1 serving	85	250

Ox
kidney, stewed	159	1 serving	25	40
liver, fried	284	1 serving	85	240
tail, stewed	250	1 serving	85	
tail, stewed with bones	89	1 serving	85	
tongue, pickled	309	1 serving	85	260

Pork
chops, grilled, lean	325	1 serving	85	275
chops, grilled, lean with bone	133	1 serving	100	133
chops, grilled, lean & fat with bone	451	1 serving	100	451

Food Category or Brand	Calories /100 g	Portion	Size /g	Calories /port
leg, roast	317	1 serving	100	317
loin, roast, lean	284	1 serving	100	284
loin, roast, lean & fat	455	1 serving	100	455
loin, salt, smoked lean	243	1 serving	100	243
Bacon				
fried, back	597	2 slices	25	150
fried, collar	438	2 slices	25	110
fried, streaky	526	2 slices	25	130
Gammon				
boiled, lean	193	1 serving	100	
boiled, lean & fat	325	1 serving	100	
rashers, fried	432	2 slices	20	
rashers, grilled	403	2 slices	20	
Ham				
boiled, lean	219	1 serving	85	185
boiled, lean & fat	435	1 serving	85	370
chopped	340	1 serving	85	290
Rabbit				
stewed	180	1 serving	85	150
stewed with bone	92	1 serving	120	110
Also see **Hare**				
Sweetbreads				
stewed	177	1 serving	85	150
Tripe				
stewed	102	1 serving	100	102
Venison				
roast	196	1 serving	85	165

Food Category or Brand	Calories /100 g	Portion	Size /g	Calories /port
Branded Meat Products				
Bejam / Iceland				
bacon burger		each		100
beef sandwich steak		each		320
chilli beef crispbake		each		195
Chinese ribsteaks	178			
corned beef crispbake		each		195
lamb grillsteak		each		205
ribsteaks	178			
Stilton & bacon chicken		each		330
Bernard Matthews				
Bar-b-ribs	246			
country grillsteaks	211			
lamb cutlet	237			
mini beef with relish	227			
Italian mini kiev		each		40
pork roast	157			
Tom Tom	227			
Bowyers				
brawn	243			
chopped ham	275			
haslet	289			
pork shoulder	161			
prime ham	161			
stuffed pork roll	325			
Butterball				
beef grillsteak		each		245
Dipper		each		60
Cherry Valley				
confit de canard	225		400	900

Food Category or Brand	Calories /100 g	Portion	Size /g	Calories /port
Mr Brain's				
faggots in rich sauce		each		130
Sainsbury's				
bacon & ham loaf	190			
black pudding	305			
corned beef roll	200			
cured pork lunch tongue	175			
cured pork shoulder	100			
English premium smoked ham	125			
English premium ham	130			
honey glazed ham	130			
honey roast ham	135			
hot dogs	225			
lean cooked ham	105			
pork lunch tongue	190			
premium corned beef	210			
roast cured pork loin	155			
roast leg of pork	150			
salt beef	135			
smoked ham	95			
York ham	280			
Waitrose				
black forest ham	252			
continental smoked ham	137			
cooked ham	171			
crumbed carving ham	185			
dry cured smoked ham	185			
farmhouse low-fat pâté	201			
Fiorucci boneless ham	253			
French country ham	122			
game pie	296			
garlic brandy pâté	153			
ham & chicken pie	190			

Food Category or Brand	Calories /100 g	Portion	Size /g	Calories /port
Leicester ham	186			
Maryland ham	134			
oven-baked ham	182			
peppered ham	148			
pork & egg pie	287			
pork satay stick	171			
prosciutto di Parma	352			
roast ham with apricots	186			
roast loin of pork	131			
smoked spiced ham	210			
spare ribs	154			
tandoori drumsticks	202			
turkey, ham, apricot pie	307			
Westphalian ham	196			

Generic Poultry

Chicken
boiled	203	1 serving	85	170
boiled, with bone	132	1 serving	100	132
roast	189	1 serving	85	160
roast, with bone	102	1 serving	100	102

Duck
roast	313	1 serving	85	265
roast, with bone	169	1 serving	100	169

Goose
roast	323	1 serving	85	275
roast, with bone	187	1 serving	100	187

Grouse
roast	172	1 serving	85	145
roast, with bone	114	1 serving	100	114

Food Category or Brand	Calories /100 g	Portion	Size /g	Calories /port
Guinea fowl				
roast	210	1 serving	85	175
roast, with bone	112	1 serving	100	112
Partridge				
roast, without bone	127	1 serving	100	127
Pheasant				
roast, without bone	134	1 serving	100	134
Pigeon				
boiled	218	1 serving	85	185
boiled, without bone	96	1 serving	120	115
roast, without bone	102	1 serving	120	120
Quail				
roast	321	whole	100	321
Turkey				
roast	195	1 serving	85	165
roast, with bone	117	1 serving	100	117

Branded Poultry Products

Bejam / Iceland				
chicken breasteak		each		200
chicken cordon bleu		each		325
chicken finger		each		45
chicken garlic bites		each		50
chicken goujons		each		70
chicken kiev		each		400
turkey nuggets		each		35
Bowyers				
chicken roll		each		168

Food Category or Brand	Calories /100 g	Portion	Size /g	Calories /port
Butterball				
drumstix		each		120
goldencrumb turkey steak		each		135
turkey breast steak		each		100
turkey cheeseburger		each		215
Cherry Valley				
crispy Peking duck	400			
duckling a l'orange	575			
Bernard Matthews				
golden drummer	246			
Italian mini kiev		each		40
Norfolk burger		each		100
turkey breast joint	128			
turkey burger	210			
turkey frying steak	124			
turkey leg roast	132			
turkey mince	132			
turkey roast joint	128			
Sainsbury's				
chicken roll	128			
cured turkey slice	145			
duck & orange pie	265			
fried chicken pie	114			
smoked turkey	111			
St Michael (Marks & Spencer)				
barbecued chicken breasts	186			
barbecued chicken drumsticks	186			
barbecued chicken thighs	271			
chicken tikka	186			
Chinese chicken drumsticks	207			
Chinese chicken thighs	246			
Chinese chicken wings	264			

Food Category or Brand	Calories /100 g	Portion	Size /g	Calories /port
Chinese-style breasts	218			
mini chicken kebabs	211			
Waitrose				
chicken pâté	207			
duck pâté	297			
duck supreme pâté	409			
roast turkey breast	190			
turkey breast	132			

Nuts

Most nuts contain fat, protein and fibre. Of the more common nuts, only chestnuts contain significant amounts of carbohydrate.

Nuts contain more fat than fatty meat – a Brazil nut is almost two-thirds fat; walnuts, almonds and peanuts are half fat; and hazelnuts and the fleshy part of coconut are one-third fat. Nuts are, therefore, very high in calories. Although amounts vary, about 25 per cent of the fat in nuts is polyunsaturated – in sunflower seeds it is 75 per cent.

Peanuts are the richest in protein at over 25 per cent – weight by weight they contain more protein than a hard cheese like Cheddar. Almonds, Brazils and walnuts, at around 20 per cent, contain weight for weight more protein than egg. However, their protein is of relatively low quality; a nut-based diet would not provide the range and quality of protein required for human life – a fact not always made clear by some advertisements for nuts. Nevertheless, all nut protein can be converted into energy, which is what concerns us here.

Honey roasted and sugar-coated nuts obviously have additional carbohydrates, and therefore more calories.

In the branded section have been included some 'mixed' assortments, some of which include raisins and other dried fruits.

Food Category or Brand	Calories /100 g	Portion	Size /g	Calories /port

Generic Nuts

Almonds
kernel	598			
kernel with shells	221			
roasted, salted	607			

Brazils
| kernel | 644 | | | |
| with shells | 289 | | | |

Cashew nuts
| roasted | 559 | | | |

Chestnuts
| kernel | 172 | | | |
| with shells | 142 | | | |

Cobs
| kernel | 398 | | | |
| with shells | 143 | | | |

Coconut
| fresh | 365 | | | |
| milk (no sugar added) | 625 | | | |

Macadamias
| roasted, salted | 696 | | | |

Monkey nuts
| kernel | 571 | | | |

Peanuts
honey roasted	520			
kernel	603			
kernel with shells	416			
roasted, salted	582			

Food Category or Brand	Calories /100 g	Portion	Size /g	Calories /port
Pecans				
roasted, salted	739			
Pistachios				
with shells	600			
Walnuts				
kernel	549			
with shells	352			

Branded Nuts

KP

Brannigans beer nuts	600	1 packet	50	300
honey roasted peanuts	590	1 packet	50	295
large peanuts & raisins	480	1 packet	100	480
mixed nuts & raisins	530	1 packet	50	265
peanuts, raisins & chocolate	480	1 packet	50	240
salt & vinegar peanuts	560	1 packet	50	280

Phileas Fogg

Shanghai nuts	515	1 packet	100	515

Planters

Bombay spiced peanuts	620	1 packet	50	310
dry roasted peanuts	590	1 packet	50	295
hickory smoked peanuts	610	1 packet	50	305
honey peanuts & cashews		1 packet	50	475
honey roasted peanuts	590	1 packet	50	295
salted peanuts	625	1 packet	40	250

Safeway

carnival mix	335	1 packet	100	335
honey roasted peanuts	520	1 packet	100	520
mixed nuts & raisins	515	1 packet	100	515
peanuts & raisins	470	1 packet	100	470

Food Category or Brand	Calories /100 g	Portion	Size /g	Calories /port
peanuts, raisins & chocolate	460	1 packet	100	460
salted roasted mixed nuts	630	1 packet	100	630

Sainsbury's
barbecue roasted peanuts	586			
honey cashews & peanuts	596			
luxury nut selection	607			
mixed nuts & raisins	461			
natural peanuts & raisins	404			
peanuts, raisins & chocolate	461			
peanuts & raisins	446			
salted mixed nuts	596			
tropical nut mix	350			

St Michael (Marks & Spencer)
dry roasted peanuts	586			
peanuts & raisins	414			
pistachios	600			
roasted salted cashews	579			
roast salt macadamias	696			
roasted salted nut selection	579			
roast salted pecans	739			
spicy Oriental peanuts	600			
tikka, crunchy peanuts	535			

LUXURY
fruit & nut assortment	473	1 packet	150	710
honey salted nut assortment	577	1 packet	150	865
luxury nut assortment	683	1 packet	150	1024
nut & fruit assortment	520	1 packet	150	780

Sun-Pat
salted peanuts	615			

Tee Gee
dry roasted peanuts	590	1 packet	100	590
hickory smoked almonds	510	1 packet	85	433

Food Category or Brand	Calories /100 g	Portion	Size /g	Calories /port
honey roasted peanuts	520	1 packet	100	520
mixed nut & fruit	530	1 packet	100	530
peanut kernels	595	1 packet	100	595
salted peanuts	610	1 packet	100	610
sunflower seeds	740	1 packet	125	925
Tesco				
blanched peanuts & raisins	411			
cashew nuts	600			
monkey nuts, shelled	571			
natural roast peanuts	585			
peanut kernels	571			
salted mixed nuts	621			
sesame nut crunch	560			
Waitrose				
exotic fruit & nuts	445			
fruit, nuts & seeds	475			
mixed nuts & raisins	521			
peanuts & raisins	475			

Processed Meats
Sausages, Salamis and Pâtés

Sausages are made from meat, cereal (including bread) and seasonings. The traditional sausage casing is an animal product, but artificial cases also exist. Pork sausages must contain 65 per cent meat, beef sausages 50 per cent. Frankfurters and salami, unless sold canned, must contain 85 per cent meat; the canned versions can go down to 70 per cent meat.

There are no regulations about the amount of fat the 'meat' contains. A regular grilled pork sausage is about 25 per cent fat, 13 per cent protein and slightly less carbohydrate. The rest is water. In a 'low-fat' version the fat element is down to about 14 per cent, the protein proportion moves up to 16 per cent and the carbohydrate 12 per cent. In both cases the fats are either mostly saturated or monounsaturated. Because beef sausages usually have a higher proportion of cereal, weight for weight they contain less fat than pork sausage.

Grilling eliminates between a quarter and a third of the fat. As a result, weight for weight grilled 'regular fat' and 'low-fat' sausages may end up with about the same calorific value. However, the low-fat sausage is still healthier because of the fats lost in its processing.

Frying is not all that different from grilling – almost the same amount of fat is lost.

Salamis and other continental sausages eaten cold often have very high proportions of fat, sometimes in excess of 45 per cent. Carbohydrate is low — less than 2 per cent — protein is 20 per cent and there is usually far less water (under 30 per cent) than in other types of sausage. The fats are solid and therefore very low in polyunsaturates. This explains why there can be 500 kcal in just 100 g of these sausages.

Pâtés and liver sausages are usually between 25 and 30 per cent fat, although certain types of pâté may have up to 45 per cent fat. Pâtés tend to be moister than salamis, of course, with a water content of over 50 per cent. They contain around 12 to 14 per cent protein and there is almost no carbohydrate. The vast bulk of the fats are saturated. 'Reduced fat' pâtés often show very significant reductions — one manufacturer's regular Brussels pâté is 29 per cent fat, the fat-reduced version only 12 per cent. As a result the calorific value falls from 325 kcal/100 g down to 195 kcal/100 g.

There is no legal distinction between spreads, pastes and pâtés; the cheaper items tend to have a higher proportion of non-meat filler and/or fats as opposed to meat flesh.

Food Category or Brand	Calories /100 g	Portion	Size /g	Calories /port
Generic Processed Meats				
beef sausage, fried	287	1 serving	85	245
black sausage	286	1 serving	85	240
frankfurters, canned	220	1 serving	100	220
frankfurters, cooked	303	1 serving	85	255
pork sausage, fried	326	1 serving	85	275
salami, cooked	310	1 serving	85	265
salami, dry	449	1 serving	50	220

Food Category or Brand	Calories /100 g	Portion	Size /g	Calories /port

Branded Processed Meats

Bejam/Iceland

economy thick pork		each		148
economy thick pork & beef		each		115
jumbo pork & beef		each		281
low-fat thick pork		each		93
premium pork		each		198
thick beef		each		144
thick pork		each		144
thick pork & beef		each		150
thick pork & herbs		each		135
thin pork		each		72
thin pork & beef		each		75

Bowyers

garlic sausage	304
luncheon sausage	282

Budgens

garlic sausage	206
La Rochelle Brussels Pâté	340
La Rocheele low-fat Brussels Pâté	211
pepperoni	430
pork & beef sausages	282
thin-sliced ham	97

Mattesons

black pudding	354
bratwurst	336
frankfurters	354
garlic German	248
ham	142
liver	265

Food Category or Brand	Calories /100 g	Portion	Size /g	Calories /port
Ross				
pork 8s	340	each		200
pork & beef 8s	285	each		170
pork & beef jumbo 8s	285	each		340
Safeway				
country style pork	380			
Cumberland	333			
hot & spicy	375			
pork	358			
pork & beef	323			
pork & fried onion	374			
pork & herb	357			
premium beef	339			
premium pork	380			
premium pork 90% meat	391			
Sainsbury's				
beef		each		160
Cumberland pork		each		180
Danish salami	575			
large pork & beef		each		125
liver sausage chubb	260			
low-fat pork		each		100
party pork & bacon		each		45
party pork & beef		each		45
pork		each		210
pork & beef		each		180
premium pork with herbs		each		65
skinless pork		each		100
skinless pork & beef		each		75
sliced ham sausage	150			
snack salami		each		135
FROZEN				
Lincolnshire pork, thick	310	each		155

Food Category or Brand	Calories /100 g	Portion	Size /g	Calories /port
Lincolnshire pork, thin	315	each		45
low-fat	235	each		100
pork & beef, thick	295	each		165
pork & beef, thin	295	each		80
pork economy, thick	290	each		160
pork economy, thin	340	each		85
premium pork & herb	275	each		155
premium pork, thick	280	each		155
DELI				
black pudding	229			
Danish salami	546			
frankfurter, large		each		210
frankfurter, small		each		70
pork, breakfast	246			
smoked pork, garlic	225			
St Michael (Marks & Spencer)				
beef	375			
frankfurters	295			
pork & beef	370			
pork & beef, skinless	250			
pork cocktail	350			
pork, low-fat	180			
prize-winning pork	268			
schinken pastete	252			
sliced Scottish lorne	355			
top-quality	400			
Waitrose				
beef	229			
chipolata	326			
Cotswold pork	240			
Cumberland pork	273			
Cumberland pork chipolatas	320			
Danish salami	520			

Food Category or Brand	Calories /100 g	Portion	Size /g	Calories /port
garlic salami	352			
garlic sausage	262			
German salami	427			
mild garlic sausage	277			
pepper salami	427			
pork	287			
pork & beef	335			
pork & beef chipolatas	335			
pork cocktail	287			
pork, large	159			
premium beef	229			
premium pork	310			
premium pork chipolatas	310			
smoked pork	328			
spiced pork	292			
strong garlic sausage	280			
Suffolk	254			
thick pork	270			
thin pork	275			
Walls				
light & lean country	198			
light & lean premium	178			
Lincolnshire		each		113
pork & beef	282			

Ready-made Meals

What are called here 'ready-made meals' are those substantial dishes you can buy at the supermarket, sold either frozen or chilled, which need simple heating. In some cases the identical dish is sold both chilled (for eating almost immediately) and frozen (for longer-term storage). In the listings we have grouped together canned meals; fresh, frozen and chilled meals; pies and pastries; and lunch/snack bowls and pot meals.

Increasingly the range is including a number of ethnic dishes, prepared with an increasing amount of authenticity. See also the **Meat and Poultry, Rice, Pasta and Pizza, and Vegetarian Dishes** sections.

Dishes with identical names but different brand labels may be made from very different recipes. Although it is an open secret that some well-known food manufacturers make 'own-brand' products for rival supermarkets as well as selling goods under their own name, that does not mean that they will use the same recipes; indeed, every one of the UK's main supermarket chains imposes its own very high standards.

It is with ready-made dishes that 'guessing calories by looking' becomes most difficult. Dishes based on pies, flans, pasta and rice will be relatively high in carbohydrates. In the case of pies and flans — and Indian samosas — the pastry will also contain fats.

Breaded dishes will also have plenty of carbohydrates, there will be fat in the binder, and if the breaded dish is then fried as opposed to grilled, fat will be absorbed during the cooking process. Pancake-based dishes are similar. Rice-based dishes will have the lowest amount of fats.

Although meat dishes should be relatively high in protein, there may be considerable amounts of fat not only in sausage- and mince-based dishes, but also in pies, pasties and stews.

Many sauces are based on cream or cheese – these will add considerably to the fat content and the fat itself will be low in polyunsaturates. Some tomato sauces contain surprising amounts of sugar.

Neither freezing nor canning has any direct effect on the calorific value of dishes; other nutritional qualities, however, notably vitamins, may be lost.

Microwaving and grilling cooking methods are preferable to frying. However, as a general health warning, particular care should be taken with microwaving chilled dishes – uneven cooking can result in cold spots where food has been inadequately heated and may therefore be unsafe.

Food Category or Brand	Calories /100 g	Portion	Size /g	Calories /port
Canned Meals				
Baxters				
boeuf bourgignon	98			
coq au vin	77			
Campbells				
beef stew	70			
chicken stew	79			
sausage casserole	111			
vegetable casserole	60			
Co-op				
beef casserole	73			
chilli con carne	159			

Food Category or Brand	Calories /100 g	Portion	Size /g	Calories /port
Irish stew	80			
steak & kidney pie	314			
vegetable curry	84			
Fray Bentos				
beef curry		can		109
bolognese		can		98
chilli con carne		can		114
mild chicken curry		can		79
Heinz				
baked beans with burgerbites		can		199
baked beans & mini sausages		can		270
curried beans with sultanas		can		213
Sainsbury's				
beef curry	106	½ can	212	225
chicken in white wine sauce	160	can	206	330
chilli con carne	105	½ can	213	225
Irish stew	85	½ can	213	180
sweet and sour chicken	85	½ can	213	181
St Michael (Marks & Spencer)				
chicken masala	140			
lamb provençale with potatoes	106			
minced beef & potatoes	103			
pork spare ribs in a barbecue sauce	190			
tinned beef goulash	106			

Fresh, frozen & Chilled Meals

Birds Eye Wall's				
chicken & mushroom casserole		pack		165
chicken biryani		pack		555
chilli con carne with rice		pack		425
cod mornay		pack		485

Food Category or Brand	Calories /100 g	Portion	Size /g	Calories /port
macaroni cheese		pack		415
meatballs & mashed potato				
with onion gravy		pack		425
minced beef/veg & gravy				
& potato		pack		380
roast beef platter		pack		405
roast turkey platter		pack		335
sausage & mash		pack		505
sweet & sour chicken & rice		pack		400
vegetable curry with rice		pack		460
HEALTHY OPTIONS				
beef stroganoff		pack		440
chicken & broccoli lasagne		pack		320
chicken in red wine		pack		325
lean beef lasagne		pack		335
tandoori chicken		pack		455
tuna italienne		pack		285
Boots				
beef bourgignon with rice		pack		350
beef madras with rice		pack		402
chicken korma with				
spiced pilau rice		pack		436
sweet & sour pork with				
Chinese style rice		pack		324
SHAPERS				
beef lasagne		pack		299
chicken & asparagus bake		pack		294
chicken casserole		pack		184
chicken curry		pack		263
chicken supreme		pack		255
cod & prawn bake		pack		275
ham & mushroom lasagne		pack		282
italienne chicken		pack		268

Food Category or Brand	Calories /100 g	Portion	Size /g	Calories /port
tuna & pasta bake		pack		246
lamb korma		pack		244
vegetable gratin		pack		290
Co-op				
beef stew & dumplings	119			
cauliflower cheese	135			
chicken korma	123			
chicken tikka masala with pilau rice	205			
chilli con carne & rice	113			
cottage pie	101			
cowboys dinner	112			
ranch time lunch	93			
rogan josh	123			
sausage casserole	147			
toad in the hole	222			
Ross Young's				
Caribbean chicken	74			
Chinese special rice	116			
cod crumble	179			
deep dish lasagne	151			
fish mornay	137			
Japanese beef Oriental	65			
Lancashire hot pot	102			
Ocean Classic's paella	94			
Ocean Classic's seafood crumble	197			
ocean pie	117			
Safeway				
bean & cheese enchilladas	155	pack	320	496
beef madras curry	155	pack	225	349
chinese chicken & pineapple	90	pack	340	306
hotpot	71	pack	454	322

Food Category or Brand	Calories /100 g	Portion	Size /g	Calories /port
Indian style chicken stir fry	107	pack	340	364
— lamb & apple bake	124	pack	340	422
liver & bacon	125	pack	400	500
macaroni cheese with ham	146			
salmon & dill kapli	113	pack	340	384
sliced roast beef in gravy	92	pack	227	209
vegetable stir fry with beef	66	pack	340	224

Sainsbury's

beef stew & dumplings	122	pack	300	365
bombay potato	68	½ pack	340	230
cappelletti milanese	74	pack	320	430
cheese cannelloni	158	pack	260	410
chicken tikka	104	pack	340	355
chicken tikka makhani	171	½ pack	340	580
chilli con carne	73	pack	300	220
lamb rogan josh	135			
lamb casserole	132	pack	300	395
minced beef crispbakes	100	each	180	180
6 onion bhajia	235			
Oriental hot and sour pork with rice	145	pack	315	457
Oriental Indian turkey korma with pilau rice	140			
Oriental Malaysian chicken satay with rice	160	pack	315	504
Peking crispy duck	124	½ pack	390	485
penne quatro formaggi	175	pack	320	550
saute potato with bacon and egg	160	pack	485	776
toad in the hole	241	pack	170	410
vegetable lasagne	117	pack	300	350

St Michael (Marks & Spencer)

aromatic crispy duck	224			

Food Category or Brand	Calories /100 g	Portion	Size /g	Calories /port
cannelloni	130			
chicken cordon bleu	219			
chicken dhansak	138			
chicken kiev	269			
chicken tikka masala	197			
lamb passanda	164			
lasagne	144			
noodles with sweet & sour pork	131			
prawn rogan josh	80			
prawns with spring onion & ginger	131			
Thai noodles	139			
Thai peanut chicken curry	181			
Thai satay	196			
toad in the hole	255			
vegetable thali	131			
Waitrose				
beef tostadas	207			
cannelloni di carne	144			
chicken pasanda	185			
chicken patia	114			
chicken vindaloo	117			
Chinese egg fried rice	163			
Chinese stir fry	97			
Cumberland pie	110			
gobi aloo	85			
lemon pilau	189			
pasta & vegetable bake	99			
potato & corned beef bake	106			
salmon & pasta bake	119			
tagliatelli niçoise	162			
veg curry	58			
veg kofta makhawala	152			

Food Category or Brand	Calories /100 g	Portion	Size /g	Calories /port
vegetable moussaka	149			
vegetable shepherds pie	76			

Weight Watchers from Heinz

beef cannelloni				250
beef Oriental with special egg rice				281
chicken korma with pullao rice				280
chicken morengo with rice				272
Indonesian nasi goreng				268
Malaysian hot & sour beef with rice				280
Thai prawn molee with rice				265
vegetable hot pot				238

Pies and Pastries

Birds Eye Wall's

chicken pie		pie		270
steak & kidney pie		pie		261
turkey & ham pie		pie		276

Boots

cheese & onion rolls		pack		335
chicken, sweetcorn & mushroom pasty		pack		286
chicken, vegetable & cheese pasty		pack		273
ratatouille cheese topped pie		pack		277
traditional Cornish pasty		pack		466

Co-op

chicken satay flan	195			
corned beef flan	253			
deep-filled chicken & vegetable pie	218			
deep-filled quorn & mushroom pie	248			

Food Category or Brand	Calories /100 g	Portion	Size /g	Calories /port
flan quorn & leek	242			
meat & potato pie	275			
pork pie	390			
potato, cheese & onion pasty	267			
quiche/egg, cheese & onion flan	213			
sausage rolls (5)	413			
wholemeal provençale quiche	232			
vegetable pasty	293			
Ross Young				
Cornish pasties	228			
family chicken & vegetable	232			
family steak & kidney	270			
minced beef & onion	276			
minced beef & onion pasties	259			
Sainsbury's				
beef & onion pasty		pasty		395
bombay potato pasty		pasty		370
chicken, ham & broccoli roll		½ roll		445
chicken & vegetable		pie		335
crusty bake pork		pie		480
deep-filled steak		pie		460
deep-filled steak & kidney		pie		530
exhibition lattice pork		¼ pie		405
minced beef & onion		¼ pie		320
pork sausage rolls		roll		125
steak & kidney pudding		roll		365
vegetable roll		½ roll		415

St Michael (Marks & Spencer)

CUMBERLAND PIES

chicken & broccoli	105			
vegetable	107			

Food Category or Brand	Calories /100 g	Portion	Size /g	Calories /port
DEEP-FILLED				
chicken & leek	232			
steak & onion	240			
FLAKEY				
lamb & vegetable (2)	215			
minced beef roll	297			
OVAL PUFF				
chicken & vegetable	237			
vegetable & cheese	269			
PASTIES				
beef & onion	263			
cheese & onion	305			
ham & cheese	293			
traditional cornish	271			
PLATE				
roast chicken	278			
roast turkey & ham	240			
steak & kidney	289			
PUDDINGS AND ROLL				
steak & kidney	213			
SHORTCRUST				
beefsteak pies (2)	280			
chicken	263			
TOPCRUST				
beefsteak	242			
Waitrose				
cheese & ham lattice bake	287			
chicken & asparagus pie	296			
chunky steak pie	221			
Melton Mowbray pork pie	389			

Food Category or Brand	Calories /100 g	Portion	Size /g	Calories /port
minced beef & onion pie	279			
rainbow trout pie	287			
salmon & broccoli pie	291			
salmon & cucumber quiche	256			
steak & kidney pie	272			
trout & soured cream flan	270			
venison, mushroom & beef pie	237			

Lunch/Snack Bowls and Pot Meals

Boots

SHAPERS SNACKPOTS
pasta bolognese		136
beef chow mein		156
pasta carbonara		231

SHAPERS MICROWAVEABLE POT MEALS
lamb hot pot		138
tortellini		143
tuna & pasta		233

SNACKPOTS/POTMEALS
Oriental chicken		175
macaroni provençal		153

Golden Wonder

POT LIGHT
spicy chicken	65	pot	194
Chinese chicken	64	pot	191

POT NOODLE
beef & tomato		pot	288
cheese & tomato		pot	265
chicken & mushroom		pot	289
spicy curry		pot	308

Food Category or Brand	Calories /100 g	Portion	Size /g	Calories /port
sweet & sour		pot		269
POT RICE				
chicken curry		pack		265

Heinz

LUNCHBOWL
beef curry with rice				194
beef goulash with noodles				188
chilli con carne with rice				214
country vegetable casserole				110
lamb & vegetable casserole				202
pasta shells in cheese & tomato sauce				212
spaghetti hoops with mini sausages				257
sweet & sour pork with rice				233

MICROWAVE LUNCHBOX
coq au vin				262
Mexican chicken				205
Oriental chicken with hoi sin sauce				218
vegetable tikka masala				240

Microchef Snacks
beans & burgers				261
beef casserole				145
chicken curry				212

Rice, Pasta and Pizza

Rice

Rice is mostly carbohydrate in the form of starch; brown rice has more protein than white since only the outer husk of the plant has been removed. There are also very small quantities of oil in rice, about half of which is polyunsaturated.

Raw white rice is 11 per cent water; by the time it has been cooked the proportion of water is between 65 and 70 per cent. Differences in the calorific value of various types of dried rice — basmati, pilau, Italian — usually depend on the amount of moisture in the grain. The different types of grain also absorb water in the cooking process to varying extents, and this too can result in apparently anomalous calorific values.

Rice is usually boiled but is also fried; however, in most frying processes only small amounts of oil are absorbed. For the health-conscious it is better to fry in oils than in solid fats; in Indian cooking *ghee* — clarified butter — is used. Chinese fried rice may also contain egg — this will then increase the amounts of fat and cholesterol; however the overall dish would still be categorized as low in fats.

Prepared rice dishes — or side-dishes — containing vegetables will have, weight for weight, lower energy values than portions of rice alone. Also see the sections on **Ethnic Foods** and **Ready-made Meals**.

Pasta

Basic pasta is made from milled durum wheat and water, which is made into a dough and then rolled, shaped and cut. It is now widely sold 'fresh' as well as in the traditional dried form. This means that nutritional data as it appears on a pack may be for cooked pasta — when it will have absorbed large quantities of water — for uncooked fresh, or uncooked dry. Raw 'dried' pasta still has a water content of 9 or 10 per cent; by the time it is cooked the water content is above 70 per cent. A fresh pasta has a moisture content of about 30 per cent.

In a dry pasta most of the energy is in the form of carbohydrate — as starch — and will be about 75 per cent of the total content. Protein will be about 12 per cent and fat 2 per cent. Some pasta — tagliatelle, for example — is made with egg, the main effect being to increase the fat content to 8–10 per cent.

A simple pasta sauce of tomatoes and minced meat will have a much lower calorific value than one containing eggs or olive oil, or where the dish has been liberally sprinkled with Parmesan cheese (see the section on **Dairy Products**).

One manufacturer's canned spaghetti bolognese may be quite different from another's, and again one brand of chilled or frozen lasagne may have a very different calorific value than another. Even 'tomato sauce' can vary considerably, depending on the amount of sugar used in it. The table below will give you an idea of the range.

We have also included some pasta sauces. A few pasta-related dishes also appear in the **Ready-made Meals** section.

Pizza

Pizza dough is principally carbohydrate in the form of starch. The classic pizza covering is tomato sauce and cheese — the margharita — plus various possible additions. A typical pizza of this type is just over 50 per cent water, 25 per cent carbohydrate (of which 2 to 3 per cent will be sugars), 9 per cent protein and 12 per cent fat. Just under half the fat will be saturated and will come mostly from the cheese.

Deep-pan and 'French bread' pizzas have, weight for weight, lower energy values, higher proportions of carbohydrate and lower proportions of fats than more traditional thin-crust pizzas.

The pizzas listed are 'ready-made' dishes that you heat/cook yourself. Some are deep-frozen (listed as 'frozen' in this table), others will be found in your supermarket's chill cabinet. You can use the data given here as the basis for estimating the calorie content of pizzas you make yourself from basic ingredients or those you eat in restaurants.

Information about favourite products from the popular pizza restaurant chains can be found in the **Fast Foods** section, while information about other Italian specialities appear in the **Ethnic Foods** section.

Food Category or Brand	Calories /100 g	Portion	Size /g	Calories /port

Generic Rice

Basmati
| boiled | 225 | | | |
| raw | 357 | | | |

Brown & Wild
| raw | 325 | | | |

Caribbean
| cooked | 125 | | | |
| raw | 500 | | | |

Food Category or Brand	Calories /100 g	Portion	Size /g	Calories /port
Easy-cook				
cooked	138			
Pilau (Pilaff)				
boiled	220			
raw	350			
Pudding rice				
cooked	95			
Quick-cook				
cooked	125			
Quinoa				
raw	346			
Risotto				
cooked	180			
White, polished				
boiled	100			
Wholegrain brown				
cooked	160			

Branded Rice

Batchelors Savoury

beef		per packet	435
chicken		per packet	440
Chinese chicken, fried		per packet	615
Chinese special, fried		per packet	580
Chinese sweet & sour		per packet	640
golden or mushroom		per packet	445
hot Indian		per packet	665
Indian special, fried		per packet	660
mild curry		per packet	425
Mediterranean		per packet	540

Food Category or Brand	Calories /100 g	Portion	Size /g	Calories /port
tandoori special, fried		per packet		635
wholegrain mixed vegetable		per packet		425
Co-op Savoury				
beef or mushroom		per packet		435
chicken curry		per packet		430
mixed vegetable		per packet		425
Countrywild				
raw	325			
Froqual				
egg-fried		per packet		450
golden savoury		per packet		355
mushroom		per packet		365
Ross				
Chinese special	121	1 serving	120	145
stir-fry rice mix	71	1 serving	120	85
Sainsbury's				
brown, canned		1 can	425	420
St Michael (Marks & Spencer)				
chicken-style		156	400	615
Indian		135	400	540
Thai coconut	200	1 serving	120	240
Tesco				
mild curry rice, raw	314			
mild curry rice, cooked	106			
mixed vegetable rice, raw	316			
mixed vegetable rice, cooked	111			
Tilda				
easy cook US long-grain, raw	335			

Food Category or Brand	Calories /100 g	Portion	Size /g	Calories /port
Uncle Ben's				
broccoli, au gratin	136	1 serving	120	163
Indian rice	125	1 serving	120	150
long grain & wild	114	1 serving	120	136
mushroom royale	125	1 serving	120	150
paprika provençale	125	1 serving	120	150
quick cook, raw	342			
Generic Dried Pasta				
macaroni	360	1 serving	75	270
noodles	364	1 serving	75	273
spaghetti	365	1 serving	75	274
spirals, wholewheat	275	1 serving	75	206
twists	344	1 serving	75	258
Generic Fresh Pasta				
capelliti	156	1 serving	75	117
ravioli	318	1 serving	75	239
tagliatelle	156	1 serving	75	117
tortelloni, five-cheese	304	1 serving	75	228
Branded Pasta				
Bejam/Iceland				
boiled pasta mix	57			
mixed vegetables with pasta spirals	68			
Birds Eye				
vegetable pasta	86			
Boots				
pasta carbonara		1 pot		230

Food Category or Brand	Calories /100 g	Portion	Size /g	Calories /port
Buitoni				
cannelloni	97	1 can	215	222
wholewheat ravioli	84	1 can	215	181
Co-op				
spaghetti in tomato sauce	58	1 can	410	240
wholewheat spaghetti in				
tomato sauce	58	1 can	410	240
Crosse & Blackwell				
Alphabetti spaghetti		1 can	425	255
Fred Bear beans & pasta		1 can	440	360
higher-fibre spaghetti		1 can	425	255
spaghetti rings		1 can	213	140
straight spaghetti		1 can	213	140
wholewheat spaghetti		1 can	213	130
Findus				
cannelloni	119	1 serving	200	238
lasagne	121	1 serving	242	292
Heinz				
Haunted House	73	1 can	215	155
macaroni cheese		1 can	210	205
Noodle Doodles		1 can	215	125
ravioli in beef & tomato sauce		1 can	215	165
ravioli in tomato sauce	74	1 can	215	165
spaghetti bolognese	89	1 can	210	185
spaghetti hoops		1 can	215	135
spaghetti with sausages	123	1 can	215	265
spaghetti in tomato sauce	65	1 can	215	135
Weight Watchers spaghetti		1 can	215	115
KP				
bolognaise quick lunch		1 tub		150

Food Category or Brand	Calories /100 g	Portion	Size /g	Calories /port
Morton				
mushroom tortellini		1 can	410	325
pasta with bacon		1 can	410	420
pasta shells bolognese		1 can	410	320
pasta twists with tuna		1 can	410	415
Napolina				
ravioli in tomato and beef sauce		1 can	411	370
ravioli in tomato sauce		1 can	411	350
Ross				
lasagne	120			
macaroni cheese	110			
Safeway				
macaroni cheese	118	1 can	215	254
ravioli		1 can	200	160
spaghetti in tomato sauce	59	1 can	215	127
Sainsbury's				
lasagne pescatore	450			
ravioli	81	1 can	215	174
spaghetti	56	1 can	215	120
spaghetti bolognese	130	1 serving	200	260
tagliatelle	130	1 serving	200	260
St Michael (Marks & Spencer)				
lasagne	136	1 serving	75	102
pasta & vegetable bake	104	per pack		295
seafood fettucine	186	per pack	350	650
Waitrose				
fish lasagne	116	1 serving	200	232
ravioli	83	1 can	215	178
spaghetti in tomato sauce	55	1 can	215	118
tagliatelle niçoise	170	1 serving	200	340
vegetable lasagne	106	1 serving	200	212

Food Category or Brand	Calories /100 g	Portion	Size /g	Calories /port
Whole Earth				
garden vegetable	225	per pot		
savoury noodle	240	per pot		

Pasta Sauces

Ragu

broccoli & white wine	62	jar		273
courgette & aubergine	50	jar		220
parmesan style	90	jar		396
red wine & herbs	84	jar		370
traditional	79	jar		348

Sainsbury's

FRESH

bolognese		½ pack		166
carbonara		½ pack		274
napoletana		½ pack		100
pesto		½ pack		346

St Michael (Marks & Spencer)

FRESH

carbonara	213			
pesto	498			
tomato & masacarpone	127			

Branded Pizza

Bejam/Iceland

| cheese & tomato | | 1 pizza | | 234 |
| ham & mushroom | | 1 pizza | | 225 |

Birds Eye

French bread pizza		1 pizza		330
ham & mushroom	242	1 pizza	265	640
Pizza Deluxe		1 pizza		360

Food Category or Brand	Calories /100 g	Portion	Size /g	Calories /port
tomato & cheese	278	1 pizza	227	630
tomato & cheese, luxury	290	1 pizza	93	270

Findus

CRISPY BASE

cheese & tomato	208			
ham	168			

FRENCH BREAD

bacon, peppers & mushroom	192			
Italian sausage	183			
savoury barbecue	223			
tomato & cheese	228			

FROZEN

barbecue beef		1 pizza		400
ham & pineapple	188	1 pizza	170	320

Marietta's

mushroom		1 pizza		520
pizza fingers		1 finger		95
special		1 pizza		610
tomato & cheese snack		1 snack		210

McVitie's

pizza pie		1 pizza		440

Ross

cheese & onion	210	1 pizza		190
crispy bacon	250	1 pizza		230
French bread pizza	270	1 pizza		380
ham, mushroom & cheese	220	1 pizza		200
tomato & cheese	220	1 pizza		200
wholemeal tomato & cheese	237	1 pizza		210

Safeway

DEEP-PAN

Swiss cheese & ham	246			

Food Category or Brand	Calories /100 g	Portion	Size /g	Calories /port
tomato, cheese & ham	198			
FRESH				
cheese, tomato, ham & mushroom	206			
cheese, tomato, mushroom & onion	215			
cheese, tomato & pepper	206			
FROZEN				
cheese & onion	233			
cheese & tomato	247			
ham & mushroom	227			
luxury, pepperoni	205			
luxury, tuna & prawn	198			
Sainsbury's				
AMERICAN STYLE				
cajun chicken	208	½	205	412
chilli beef	921	½	220	439
BOBLI				
bacon & mushroom		½	175	347
cheeseburger		½	173	421
CHICAGO STYLE				
ham & mushroom		½	205	443
vegetable provençale		½	215	501
FOCACCIA DEEP & CRISPY				
cheese & tomato		½	230	543
garlic, cheese & onion		½	182	748
St Michael (Marks & Spencer)				
American cheese & tomato	212			
tomato, cheese & onion	203			

Food Category or Brand	Calories /100 g	Portion	Size /g	Calories /port
Waitrose				
Campagnola	164			
Mariana	179			
pepperoni	189			
FRENCH BREAD				
ham & mushroom	201			
tomato & cheese	220			
PAN-BAKED				
cheese & tomato	222			
chilli con carne	222			

Sandwiches

Sandwiches are often thought of as snacks, but that doesn't mean they're necessarily low in calories. Those that contain mayonnaise or other oil- or dairy-rich sauces (see **Dairy Products** and **Fats and Oils**) may be very high-calorie indeed.

The sandwiches listed here are the types sold chilled and sealed in clear plastic cases. The life of this type of sandwich is prolonged by the use of inert gases sealed into the package, which keep oxygen out and thereby keep the sandwich fresher longer.

Unwrapped sandwiches sold in other outlets will have similar calorific values, though in general the sealed sandwiches tend to have more substantial fillings.

Also see the section on **Bread**.

Food Category or Brand	Calories /100 g	Portion	Size /g	Calories /port
Branded Sandwiches				
Asda				
bacon, tomato & lettuce		each		205
cheese & roast ham		each		197
coronation chicken		each		252
egg mayonnaise & cress		each		209
ham salad roll		each		243
ploughmans traditional		each		276
poached salmon		each		217

Food Category or Brand	Calories /100 g	Portion	Size /g	Calories /port
prawn mayonnaise		each		167
roast beef & salad		each		149
roast chicken & lettuce		each		191
roast ham		each		174
smoked chicken & bacon		each		257
smoked ham & emmental		each		265
tuna with lettuce		each		181

Boots

BAPS

corned beef, tomato & American-styled mustard		each		352
German salami & soft cheese		each		519

GOURMET SANDWICH RANGE

blue brie & bacon with Chinese leaf, endive & radicchio		each		442
crab pâté with crumbled egg		each		463
spicy Jamaican chicken		each		395
stilton, celery & apple with a mild port dressing		each		489

NEW YORK STYLE BAGELS

pastrami & tomato with mustard mayonnaise		each		281
Shapers ham & cheese		each		199
smoked salmon & egg		each		313

REGULAR SANDWICHES

bacon, lettuce & tomato with mayonnaise		each		450
beef, green pepper & blackbean mayonnaise		each		323
egg & bacon/mature cheddar & pickle/prawn mayonnaise		each		664
egg & bacon with mayonnaise		each		582

Food Category or Brand	Calories /100 g	Portion	Size /g	Calories /port
egg mayonnaise & cress		each		312
farmhouse lunch — mature				
cheddar, pickle, onion & salad		each		351
mature cheddar cheese & coleslaw		each		585
prawn mayonnaise and lettuce		each		548
roast chicken salad/ham, cheese				
& pineapple/prawns &				
fromage frais		each		385
smoked ham, chicken &				
coleslaw		each		423
smoked ham, salad &				
mustard mayonnaise		each		293
SHAPERS SANDWICHES				
chicken & Chinese leaf with				
lemon mayonnaise		each		199
chicken korma, apricot,				
almonds & Chinese leaf		each		281
Greek–style salad with				
feta and yogurt mayonnaise		each		178
poached Scottish salmon, Chinese				
leaf with mayonnaise		each		248
seafood cocktail — prawns &				
white fish in lemon mayonnaise				
& lettuce		each		229
smoked ham, soft cheese &				
pineapple with lettuce		each		196
turkey & Chinese leaf with				
sage & onion mayonnaise		each		242
TRADITIONAL SANDWICHES				
fresh chicken & stuffing		each		621
honey roast ham with salad &				
mustard in thickly sliced				
malted wholegrain bread		each		337

Food Category or Brand	Calories /100 g	Portion	Size /g	Calories /port
Safeway				
chicken italienne	190			
cream cheese, fruit & walnut	283			
egg & bacon	283			
Greek pitta	209			
ham & cheese	285			
ham & coleslaw	182			
ham & pesto	261			
peking duck	187			
ploughmans roll	276			
salami & gruyère	297			
smoked salmon & fromage frais	235			
spicy Jamaican chicken	232			
tandoori pitta	186			
Sainsbury's				
blue brie & grape		pack		417
Cheddar cheese, peppers & sweetcorn		pack		382
chicken with American-style stuffing		pack		395
chicken & bacon club		pack		408
chicken tikka		pack		452
chicken salad		pack		271
chicken salad with mayonnaise		pack		378
cottage cheese & Florida salad		pack		275
duck à l'orange		pack		456
mixed summer salad with fromage frais & chives		pack		214
pastrami on rye		pack		282
prawn & mayonnaise		pack		321
prawn & reduced-calorie mayonnaise		pack		255
roast chicken – no mayonnaise		pack		279

Food Category or Brand	Calories /100 g	Portion	Size /g	Calories /port
roast chicken & oak-smoked ham		pack		420
Scottish smoked salmon & egg		pack		434
smoked ham, cheese & pineapple		pack		265
soft cheese & cucumber		pack		332
tuna & cucumber		pack		307
vegetarian Cheddar cheese & spring onion		pack		308
TRIPLE PACKS				
bacon & tomato, chicken, double Gloucester cheese		pack		564
chicken salad, egg mayonnaise, cheese & celery		pack		619
chicken salad, red salmon & cucumber, ham & tomato		pack		344
St Michael (Marks & Spencer)				
cheese & pickle ploughmans		each		478
chicken tikka		each		366
coronation chicken		each		437
egg & cress		each		314
frankfurter & relish		each		428
ham, cheese & coleslaw		each		375
ham, cheese & pickle		each		438
ham, cheese & pickle triple		each		657
poached trout		each		382
prawn mayonnaise		each		399
prawn mayonnaise triple		each		597
roast beef & salad		each		284
roast chicken salad		each		409
salmon & cucumber		each		276
sausage & coleslaw		each		517
tuna		each		324
tuna & three-bean salad		each		428

Food Category or Brand	Calories /100 g	Portion	Size /g	Calories /port
AMERICAN STYLE				
beef Sloppy Joe		each		504
pastrami on rye		each		180
DOUBLE DECKERS				
chicken/bacon lettuce & tomato		each		432
prawn & soft cheese		each		259
LOW CALORIE				
lean Danish ham		each		240
prawn & cucumber dressing with lettuce		each		274
ROLLS				
ham roll		each		375
ploughmans roll		each		516
SELECTIONS				
fish triple		each		484

ham, cheese & pickle/chicken
  — no mayo/prawn &
  mayonnaise triple
		each		523

prawn, turkey & cheese selection		each		604
VEGETARIAN				
curried coleslaw		each		327
provençale vegetables		each		289
Waitrose				
assorted triple	324			
bacon triple pack	310			
beef, tomato & coleslaw	189			
bierwurst & cheddar	310			
Cheddar, bacon & leek	286			
cheese, carrot & nut	291			
cheese, pineapple & ham	275			

Food Category or Brand	Calories /100 g	Portion	Size /g	Calories /port
chicken, pineapple & fromage frais	182			
chicken satay	327			
chilli chicken pitta	229			
farmhouse baguette	275			
fish quarter pack	215			
free-range-egg salad	248			
fromage frais, salmon & prawns	141			
garlic & herb chicken	303			
pesto, cheese & salad	198			
salami ciabatta	324			
salmon & curd cheese	167			
tuna, celery & lemon	264			
turkey stuffing	222			
vegetarian salad	251			

Soups

Fairly obviously, soups are mostly water. Their energy component comes from carbohydrate (as starch).

Meat-based soups may contain small amounts of fat. The real trap lies in thickened soups. Potato-based thickening — as in parmentiers — adds only carbohydrate; the same is true of cornflower and ground pulses as additives — but cream and eggs will add fats and protein.

The manufacturers' figures for powdered soups are usually for the powder itself rather than the cooked (and very much diluted) soup. The main difference between a cup soup and a conventional packet soup is cooking time.

Food Category or Brand	Calories /100 g	Portion	Size /g	Calories /port

Canned Soups

Baxters

SPECIAL OCCASION/LUXURY RANGE

Food Category or Brand	Calories /100 g	Portion	Size /g	Calories /port
beef consommé	12			
broccoli & Gruyère	56			
Chinese noodle	34			
cream of courgette	54			
cream of pheasant	60			
Cullen Skink	85			
fisherman's pottage	41			
lobster bisque	54			

Food Category or Brand	Calories /100 g	Portion	Size /g	Calories /port
TARTAN RANGE				
bean & bacon	54			
chicken broth	32			
cock-a-leekie	22			
cream of tomato	69			
french onion	24			
golden pea	58			
minestrone	30			
pea & ham	75			
royal game	32			
scotch broth	39			
VEGETARIAN SOUPS				
carrot & butter bean	47			
country garden	28			
garden pea with mint	32			
spicy parsnip	49			
tomato & orange	40			
Heinz				
beef				80
chicken & mushroom				78
cream of asparagus				101
cream of mushroom				89
cream of tomato				116
BIG SOUP				
beef & bacon hotpot				97
beef & vegetable				75
chicken & vegetable				82
thick country veg & ham				129
FARMHOUSE				
beef & vegetable				70
potato & leek				69
Scotch broth				89

Food Category or Brand	Calories /100 g	Portion	Size /g	Calories /port
PREMIUM SOUP				
beef, potato & red pepper				98
chicken, sweetcorn & asparagus				131
vegetable korma				87
SPICY				
curried chicken with rice				112
ham & pepper				75
WHOLESOUP				
farmhouse vegetable				90
ham & butter bean				106
mixed bean with herbs				128
tomato & lentil				109

Sainsbury's

Food	Calories /100 g	Portion	Size /g	Calories /port
CANNED SOUPS				
celery		½ can		110
chicken		½ can		140
cream of chicken		½ can		130
cream of tomato		½ can		150
extra thick vegetable		½ can		105
lentil with bacon		½ can		100
mulligatawny		½ can		115
mushroom		½ can		115
pea & ham		½ can		120
spicy bean & vegetable		½ can		85
spicy tomato & chick pea		½ can		
vegetable & beef		½ can		135
GOURMET SOUP				
beef consommé with sherry		½ can		25
chestnut mushroom with garlic		½ can		75
crab bisque		½ can		95
cream of broccoli		½ can		120

Food Category or Brand	Calories /100 g	Portion	Size /g	Calories /port
cream of celery & stilton		½ can		195
French onion		½ can		55
smoked trout with lemon		½ can		125
SUMMER SOUPS				
carrot & orange		½ can		56
gazpacho		½ can		70
minted pea		½ can		60
tomato & basil		½ can		100
vichyssoise		½ can		114

St Michael (Marks & Spencer)

beef & vegetable	69			
chicken & vegetable	57			
cream of chicken	68			
cream of tomato	73			
lentil & bacon	65			
mediterranean soup	37			
mushroom soup	54			
pea & ham	55			
Scotch broth	62			
winter vegetable	44			

Weight Watchers from Heinz

celery				64
chicken noodle				58
lentil & carrot				76
minestrone				53
Wholesome Soup, curried vegetable				96

Fresh Soups

New Convent Garden

ajiaco Bogotano	37	1 carton	568	
carrot & coriander	43	1 carton	568	245
celery with blue cheese & cider	44	1 carton	568	

Food Category or Brand	Calories /100 g	Portion	Size /g	Calories /port
chicken with lemon	74	1 carton	568	420
goulash soup	48	1 carton	568	
green pea & bacon	36	1 carton	568	205
lentil & winter vegetable	33	1 carton	568	185
soupe de poissons	47	1 carton	568	
spinach with nutmeg	40	1 carton	568	225
summer tomato	46	1 carton	568	260
Tuscan bean	43	1 carton	568	245
vichyssoise	39	1 carton	568	220
Sainsbury's				
creamed curry	75	1 jar	540	405
lobster bisque	33	1 jar	540	190
tomato & herb	47	1 jar	540	270
watercress	47	1 jar	540	270
St Michael (Marks & Spencer)				
cauliflower	106	1 pack	450	475
fish provençale	69	1 pack	450	310
French onion	220	1 pack	450	990
gazpacho	24	1 pack	450	110
mushroom	149	1 pack	450	670
seafood	252	1 pack	450	1135
sweetcorn chowder	93	1 pack	450	420
vichyssoise	106	1 pack	450	475
watercress	86	1 pack	450	385
winter vegetable	62	1 pack	450	280
Waitrose				
courgette & Stilton	54	1 carton	568	305
minted vichyssoise	43	1 carton	568	245
mixed vegetable	35	1 carton	568	200
Scotch broth	28	1 carton	568	160
spinach & watercress	34	1 carton	568	195
tomato & orange	43	1 carton	568	245

Food Category or Brand	Calories /100 g	Portion	Size /g	Calories /port
HOME-MADE SOUPS				
bone & vegetable broth	62	1 serving	250	155
lentil	100	1 serving	250	250
mixed	39	1 serving	250	98
potato	92	1 serving	250	230

Packet Soups

Batchelors Cup Soups

chicken & mushroom	221	1 packet		62
golden vegetable	250	1 packet		70
minestrone (with croutons)	250	1 packet		70
onion	393	1 packet		110
thick mushroom	386	1 packet		108
tomato	296	1 packet		83
vegetable & beef	307	1 packet		86

Holland & Barrett

soup mixes	285	1 packet		81

Knorr

chicken & leek	338	1 packet		233
chicken noodle	347	1 packet		187
Cornish seafood	374	1 packet		278
lentil	314	1 packet		301
minestrone	312	1 packet		243
oxtail	327	1 packet		250
pea with ham	327	1 packet		250
spring vegetable	280	1 packet		106
sweetcorn	368	1 packet		328
thick vegetable	310	1 packet		242

Sainsbury's

bacon & tomato	380	1 packet	30	108
chicken & leek	370	1 packet	30	105
chicken & mushroom	400	1 packet	30	114

Food Category or Brand	Calories /100 g	Portion	Size /g	Calories /port
chicken & sweetcorn	365	1 packet	30	104
chicken & vegetable	385	1 packet	30	109
French onion	315	1 packet	30	89
golden vegetable	350	1 packet	30	99
minestrone	340	1 packet	30	96
tomato & beef	340	1 packet	30	96
tomato & vegetable	345	1 packet	30	98

Sugar, Syrups, Confectionery and Cereal Bars

Confectionery

Chocolate is approximately 30 per cent fat and 60 per cent carbohydrate. It has very little water or protein. The main fat component is saturated fat; nearly all of the carbohydrate is sugars rather than starch.

There is hardly any difference in the calorific value of the various sorts of chocolate – brown, dark brown, white, flavoured. Most 'filled' chocolate bars have, weight for weight, a lower calorific value than solid chocolate. Milk chocolate is rather fattier than plain and also contains cholesterol.

Most 'sweets' are almost pure carbohydrate, chiefly complex sugars. They provide instant energy – hence the use of glucose tablets by athletes and those with long work schedules – but are otherwise of no nutritional value.

Cereal Bars

Despite their boast of 100 per cent natural ingredients and the undoubted benefits of the dietary fibre they contain – up to 20 per cent in some cases – cereal bars are not especially good for you. Typical calorific values are 400 to 500 kcal/100 g, of which nearly half will be carbohydrate. Half of this carbohydrate is sugar. This means that a typical 100 g bar contains 25 g of sugar – five teaspoons-full!

Protein is likely to be less than 10 per cent. Oil, usually

mostly unsaturated, will be just under 20 per cent. The 'chewy' type of bar will usually have a higher proportion of fats.

Chocolate-coated bars will have additional saturated fats and sugar. Carob coating adds over 100 kcal/100 g to the bar; yogurt coating adds 130 kcal/100 g.

If you are on a calorie-controlled diet with the aim of losing weight rather than gaining it, do yourself a favour and try to avoid everything listed in this section.

Food Category or Brand	Calories /100 g	Portion	Size /g	Calories /port
Sugar				
demerara	394			
white	394			
Syrups				
corn	289			
maple	251			
golden	297			
Generic Chocolate				
milk	588			
plain	544			
Branded Chocolate				
Aero		1 bar		250
Applause		1 bar		220
Bounty, milk		1 bar		275
Bounty, plain		1 bar		270
Crunchie		1 bar		195
Curly Wurly		1 bar		130
Dairy Milk (Cadbury's)		1 bar		255
Dime		1 bar		160
Flake		1 bar		170

Food Category or Brand	Calories /100 g	Portion	Size /g	Calories /port
Galaxy		1 bar		273
Kit Kat		1 bar (4 fingers)		245
Lion bar		1 bar		141
M & Ms		1 packet		225
M & Ms, peanut		1 packet		230
Maltesers		1 packet		191
Mars bar		1 std bar		295
Milky Way		1 bar		130
Minstrels		1 packet		244
Revels		1 packet		176
Ripple		1 bar		171
Rolo		1 tube		265
Smarties		1 tube		175
Snickers		1 bar		315
Toffee Crisp		1 bar		245
Topic		1 bar		248
Treets		1 packet		235
Twix		1 bar		263
Yorkie, almond		1 bar		325
Yorkie, milk		1 bar		345
Yorkie, raisin & biscuit		1 bar		285

Branded Sweets

Barker & Dobson

assorted toffees	393			
barley sugar	321			
buttered selection	393			
chewy mints	500			
chocolate dragées	464			
chocolate peanuts	553			
chocolate raisins	375			
cream or Devon toffee	428			

Food Category or Brand	Calories /100 g	Portion	Size /g	Calories /port
Everton mints	375			
fruit-flavoured drops	321			
fruit-flavoured jellies	303			
fruit-flavoured pastilles	250			
glacé mints	321			
liquorice caramel	428			
menthol & eucalyptus	500			
mint Imperials	393			
nut brittle	428			
old English toffee	428			
sherbet bon-bons	500			
toasted coconut marshmallows	393			
treacle toffee	428			
wine gums	178			
Bassett				
American hard gums	332			
cream rock	357			
jelly babies	325			
jelly beans	339			
liquorice allsorts	357			
mint Imperials	378			
real fruit gums	296			
real fruit pastilles	307			
wine gums	314			
Callard & Bowser Nuttall				
barley sugar		1 sweet		25
boiled sweet		1 sweet		20
Brazil nut toffee		1 sweet		40
butterscotch		1 sweet		25
dessert nougat		1 sweet		55
extra strong mint		1 sweet		5
Mintoes		1 sweet		15
treacle toffee		1 sweet		40

Food Category or Brand	Calories /100 g	Portion	Size /g	Calories /port
Dextrosol				
dextro energy tablets		1 sweet		10
Fox's				
Glacier fruit or mint		1 packet		140
Fryers				
Hacks	357			
Victory V gums	303			
Victory V lozenges	339			
Mars				
Lockets		1 packet		155
Opals		1 packet		175
Skittles		1 packet		175
Tunes		1 packet		135
Paynes				
peanut & raisin Poppets		1 packet		210
raisin Poppets		1 packet		180
Sharps				
bon-bons, all flavours		1 sweet		25
Brazil nuts		1 sweet		30
chocolate eclair		1 sweet		45
chocolate mint cream		1 sweet		40
real fruit jelly		1 sweet		30
Terry's				
sugared almonds	464			
truffle selection	486			
Trebor				
aniseed Imperials		1 sweet		20
bon-bons, all flavours		1 sweet		25
chocolate fudge		1 sweet		45
dairy fudge		1 sweet		45
jelly babies		1 sweet		20

Food Category or Brand	Calories /100 g	Portion	Size /g	Calories /port
jelly beans		1 sweet		10
mint cream fondants		1 sweet		30
raisin fudge		1 sweet		40
Turkish Delight		1 sweet		25

Trident
sugarless chewing gum		1 stick		5

Wrigley's
Doublemint		1 stick		10
Hubba Bubba, all flavours		1 stick		15
Orbit, all flavours		1 stick		10
PK, all flavours		1 pellet		5

Branded Cereal Bars

Allinson
carob–coated country		1 bar		151
carob–coated sesame		1 bar		105
sesame crunch		1 bar		115
Weateats		each		89

FRUIT BARS
banana	251	1 bar		88
fruit crunch	425	1 bar		119
fruit & nut	320	1 bar		112
muesli	308	1 bar		108
nut crunch	464	1 bar		130

Boots
coconut crunch	452			
date & muesli		1 bar		155
fruit muesli	377			
ginger pear		1 bar		150
honey crunch	344			
natural poppy seed	432			
natural sunflower	464			

Food Category or Brand	Calories /100 g	Portion	Size /g	Calories /port
oat & honey crunch	432			
Swiss-style muesli	350			
Cluster				
apple & hazelnut	381			
apricot & chocolate chip	384			
hazelnut & raisin	418			
peanut & almond	463			
Granose				
apple & date		1 bar		85
apricot date		1 bar		85
blackberry		1 bar		188
carob muesli		1 bar		145
carob pineapple		1 bar		145
cherry		1 bar		187
date		1 bar		87
date & apricot		1 bar		85
date & coconut		1 bar		102
date & nut		1 bar		95
fig & prune		1 bar		77
ginger pear		1 bar		110
hazelnut, deluxe		1 25g bar		100
hazelnut & almond		1 bar		115
lemon		1 bar		184
mixed fruit		1 bar		192
orange		1 bar		188
soft muesli apple		1 bar		104
soft muesli chocolate chip		1 bar		121
strawberry		1 bar		187
Holly Mills				
apple & cardamon	424	1 bar		170
apple & hazelnut	490	1 bar		147
apricot honey	277	1 bar		83
apricot malt	263	1 bar		79

Food Category or Brand	Calories /100 g	Portion	Size /g	Calories /port
banana fruit	345	1 bar		93
banana munch	475	1 bar		142
carob chip	490	1 bar		147
crunchy slice	492	1 bar		187
fibre-time snack	387	1 bar		147
oat, apple & raisin	441	1 bar		165
oat, apricot & almond	461	1 bar		203
oat & sesame seed	453	1 bar		135
oat & sunflower seed	455	1 bar		136
protein	416	1 bar		183
roasted peanut	520	1 bar		155
SQUARE SNACKS				
crunchy oat & nut	407	1 bar		187
muesli	432	1 bar		216
oat, fruit & nut	414	1 bar		174
Honeyrose				
apple & bran health		1 bar		60
fruit & nut		1 bar		100
Kalibu				
carob chips	493	1 bar		139
carob-coated peanuts	510	1 bar		144
carob-coated peanuts & raisins	465	1 bar		131
carob-coated raisins	431	1 bar		122
crunchy bran & raisin	432	1 bar		122
fruit & nut (no sugar)	483	1 bar		136
fruit & nut (raw sugar)	463	1 bar		131
orange (no sugar)	493	1 bar		139
orange (raw sugar)	493	1 bar		139
peanut butters	646	1 bar		182
peanut (no sugar)	507	1 bar		143
peppermint (no sugar)	493	1 bar		139
plain (no sugar)	493	1 bar		139

Food Category or Brand	Calories /100 g	Portion	Size /g	Calories /port
plain (raw sugar)	493	1 bar		139
raspberry yoghurt	411			
yoghurt break	526			
yoghurt-coated peanuts	546			
yoghurt-coated peanuts & raisins	508			
yoghurt-coated raisins	442			
SNACK BARS				
banana chew	326	1 bar		92
cherry chew	409	1 bar		115
fruit bar	338	1 bar		95
ginger fudge	414	1 bar		117
marzipan	435	1 bar		123
raisin	339	1 bar		96
Jordan's Original Crunchy Bars				
apple & bran	394	1 bar		131
coconut & honey	416	1 bar		139
honey & almonds	412	1 bar		137
orange & carob	420	1 bar		140
Mars Tracker Bars				
chocolate chip, large		1 bar		180
chocolate chip, small		1 bar		130
roasted nut, large		1 bar		185
roasted nut, small		1 bar		135
Prewetts				
apple & date dessert	257	1 bar		95
apple & ginger	333	1 bar		140
banana fruit	251	1 bar		76
carob-coated banana	305	1 bar		128
carob-coated date & fig	337	1 bar		142
carob-coated muesli	353	1 bar		148
date & fig dessert	294	1 bar		110

Food Category or Brand	Calories /100 g	Portion	Size /g	Calories /port
fruit & bran	297	1 bar		85
fruit & nut	320	1 bar		134
muesli	308	1 bar		129
orange & sultana	372	1 bar		156
Quaker				
chocolate chip, chewy		1 bar		110
fruit & nut, chewy		1 bar		110
harvest apple & raisin, chewy		1 bar		105
mint chocolate chip, chewy		1 bar		110
peanut crunch		1 bar		85
raisin crunch		1 bar		80
Sainsbury's				
fruit, bran & honey		1 bar		140
milk chocolate raisin		1 bar		90
plain chocolate apricot		1 bar		90
raisin & hazelnut		1 bar		120
St Michael (Marks & Spencer)				
apricot & almond		1 bar		95
Caribbean		1 bar		115
chocolate chip & almond		1 bar		100
chocolate chip & raisin		1 bar		95
fruit & nut		1 bar		95
Weetabix				
Alpen natural crunch		1 bar		115
apple & hazelnut		1 bar		110
apricot & chocolate chip		1 bar		110
chocolate chip & raisin		1 bar		110
orange & chocolate chip		1 bar		115

Vegetables, Pulses and Prepared Salads

Vegetables

Fresh vegetables are low in energy content; between 70 and 90 per cent of their weight is water, the small amount of carbohydrate they contain is principally starch and, with few exceptions, they are fat-free. Their nutritional benefit comes from the fact that they are great sources of vitamins, minerals and fibre.

The commonly-eaten vegetable with the highest starch is the potato: boiled potatoes are 17 per cent carbohydrate; roast potatoes 26 per cent carbohydrate and 4 or 5 per cent fat. Potatoes mashed with butter and milk will be about 15 per cent carbohydrate and 5 per cent fat.

Home-made chips (French fries) are 30 to 35 per cent carbohydrate and the fat content can be anywhere from 7 to 12 per cent; commercial frozen French fries often end up with a lower water content than home-made and as result the carbohydrate can exceed 40 per cent and the fat can be over 20 per cent. Baked oven chips usually end up at 30 per cent carbohydrate and only 4 per cent fat. In general terms thin-cut and crinkle-cut chips have a higher fat content because a greater proportion of the potato is available to be fried.

Among the more exotic vegetables, cassava and plantain are also high in starch. Plantain in particular, as it is often cooked with butter, becomes a very high-calorie dish.

Pulses

Pulses are the dried seeds of the leguminosa family of plants — that is, peas and beans. They all have a very high protein content, but for the most part this protein is the non-essential or plant-type as opposed to the essential, animal-type. The exception is the soya bean.

Pulses are a good source of B vitamins, minerals and fibre. Fresh pulses are also rich in vitamin C, but this vitamin is lost in the drying process.

Beans and pulses of all kinds are high in starch; some of the calorific values given for these are for the dried bean: dried chick peas, black-eyed peas and the like contain about 10 per cent water — after cooking the water content is between 65 and 70 per cent. In a fresh bean the water content may be over 90 per cent.

Salads

The salads covered here are the commercially-prepared kind bought in supermarkets. The fattening element usually comes from the added mayonnaise or other sauce. If you make up your own, refer to 'Vegetables' below and the section on **Fats and Oils**.

Food Category or Brand	Calories /100 g	Portion	Size /g	Calories /port
Generic Vegetables				
Ackee				
raw	154	1 serving	100	154
Agar				
canned	5	1 serving	100	5

Food Category or Brand	Calories /100 g	Portion	Size /g	Calories /port
Alfalfa Sprouts				
fresh	7	1 serving	100	7
Artichokes				
globe, boiled	7	1 head		5
Jerusalem, boiled	20	1 serving		20
Asparagus				
boiled	9	6 stalks	100	9
Aubergine				
raw	15			
Avocado				
raw (without stone)	93	whole	85	79
Bamboo Shoots				
canned	18	1 serving	85	15
Beansprouts				
canned	9	1 serving	85	7
fresh, raw	35	1 serving	85	28
Bean Threads				
dried	393	1 serving	85	334
Beetroot				
boiled	44	1 serving	80	35
raw	28			
Breadfruit				
raw	107	1 serving	85	91
Broccoli				
tops, boiled	14	1 serving	100	14
Brussels Sprouts				
boiled	16	1 serving	100	16
raw	32			

Food Category or Brand	Calories /100 g	Portion	Size /g	Calories /port
Cabbage				
red, raw	20	1 serving	85	15
savoy, boiled	9	1 serving	85	5
savoy, raw	26	1 serving	85	20
spring, boiled	8	1 serving	85	5
winter, boiled	8	1 serving	85	5
winter, raw	25	1 serving	85	20
Carrot				
canned	19	1 serving	85	16
old, boiled	19	1 serving	85	15
old, raw	23	1 serving	85	20
young, boiled	21	1 serving	85	15
Cassava				
fresh	154	1 serving	85	131
Cauliflower				
boiled	11	1 serving	85	10
raw	25	1 serving	85	21
Celeriac				
boiled	14	1 serving	85	10
Celery				
boiled	5	1 serving	85	4
raw	9	1 serving	85	5
Chicory				
raw	9			
Chinese Leaves				
boiled	18	1 serving	120	22
raw	11	1 serving	120	12
Chinese Waterchestnuts				
canned	50			

Food Category or Brand	Calories /100 g	Portion	Size /g	Calories /port
Chillies				
fresh, flesh only	21			
hot, no seeds	65			
hot, dried	338			
Chives				
raw	36	1 serving	85	33
Courgettes				
raw	18	1 serving	120	22
Cucumber				
raw	9	½ cucumber	100	9
Eggplant see Aubergine				
Endive				
raw	11			
Fennel				
boiled	11	1 serving	85	10
raw	11	1 serving	85	10
Horseradish				
raw	60			
Kale				
without stems, cooked	25	1 serving	120	28
without stems, raw	32	1 serving	120	35
Leeks				
boiled	25	1 serving	125	30
raw	30			
Lettuce				
raw	11	whole	200	20
Mangetout				
boiled	43	1 serving	120	48

Food Category or Brand	Calories /100 g	Portion	Size /g	Calories /port
raw	57	1 serving	120	
Marrow				
boiled	7	1 serving	125	10
Mint				
fresh	11	1 serving	100	
Mushrooms				
fried	217	1 serving	85	185
raw	7	1 serving	125	10
Mustard & Cress				
raw	10	1 serving	100	10
Okra				
raw	18	1 serving	120	21
Onions				
boiled	13	1 serving	85	10
fried	355	1 serving	100	355
raw	23			
spring, raw	36	6 onions	50	20
Parsley				
raw	21			
Parsnips				
boiled	56	1 serving	125	70
raw	49			
Peppers				
sweet, boiled	18	1 serving	85	15
sweet, raw	20	1 serving	85	18
Pimento				
canned	21	1 serving	100	21

Food Category or Brand	Calories /100 g	Portion	Size /g	Calories /port
Plantain				
green, boiled	125	1 serving	120	150
green, raw	114	1 serving	120	137
ripe, fried in butter	268	1 serving	120	351
Potatoes				
baked in skin (flesh only)	104	1 potato	100	105
baked in skin (with skin)	84	1 potato	150	125
boiled	80	1 potato	120	100
chips	239	1 serving	120	285
mashed (margarine & milk)	120	1 serving	150	180
new, boiled	75	1 serving	120	90
roast	123	1 serving	120	145
Pumpkin				
canned	33	pie filling	85	30
raw	15			
Radishes				
raw	15	3 radishes	45	10
Salsify				
boiled	18	1 serving	100	18
Seakale				
boiled	8	1 serving	100	8
Spinach				
boiled	26	1 serving	100	26
Spring Greens				
boiled	10	1 serving	100	10
Spring Onions				
raw	36	1 serving	100	36

Food Category or Brand	Calories /100 g	Portion	Size /g	Calories /port
Squash				
cooked, baked	67	1 serving	150	100
raw	36			
Swedes				
boiled	18	1 serving	120	20
raw	21			
Sweetcorn				
cob		whole		155
frozen	89	1 serving	120	107
Sweet Potatoes				
boiled	80	1 serving	120	95
Tomatillos				
raw	32	1 serving	120	38
Tomatoes				
fried	71	1 serving	10	7
raw	14	1 large tomato	150	20
sun-dried		1 tomato		5
Turnips				
boiled	11	1 serving	120	15
raw	18			
tops, boiled	11	1 serving	10	1
Wakame				
raw	45	1 serving	120	50
Watercress				
raw	15	1 serving	50	10
Yams				
boiled	114	1 serving	120	137
Zucchini				
see Courgettes				

Food Category or Brand	Calories /100 g	Portion	Size /g	Calories /port
Generic Pulses				
Aduki Beans				
boiled	125			
dried	275			
Baked Beans				
canned	93			
Black-eyed Peas				
dried	314			
boiled	118			
Borlotti Beans				
canned	168			
Butter Beans				
boiled	103			
dried	293			
Chick Peas				
boiled	150			
raw	325			
Flageolet				
boiled	114			
canned	114			
dried	350			
French Beans				
boiled	7			
Garbanzo Beans see Chick Peas				
Haricot Beans				
boiled	95			
dried	289			

Food Category or Brand	Calories /100 g	Portion	Size /g	Calories /port
Kidney Beans				
boiled	103			
canned	100			
dried	268			
Mung Beans				
boiled	93			
dried	282			
Peas				
canned	86			
dried, boiled	100			
dried, raw	275			
fresh, boiled	49			
fresh, raw	64			
frozen or dried	64			
split, dried, boiled	116			
split, dried, raw	303			
Pinto Beans				
boiled	139			
dried	332			
Runner Beans				
raw	15			
Soya Beans				
boiled	143			
dried	375			

Branded Prepared Salads

Safeway

apple, peach & nut	210			
brown rice	220			
cheese, celery & pineapple	180			

Food Category or Brand	Calories /100 g	Portion	Size /g	Calories /port
celery, apple & mandarin	140			
crisp vegetable	45			
mild curried rice	175			
potato, celery & dill	130			
potato, ham & Stilton	215			
sweetcorn	135			
three-bean	155			

Sainsbury's

Food Category or Brand	Calories /100 g	Portion	Size /g	Calories /port
apple, peach & nut	210			
beetroot	90			
Bombay potato	85			
celery, nut & sultana	245			
coleslaw	155			
coleslaw with cheese	195			
coleslaw with prawns	140			
coleslaw with low-calorie dressing	105			
Florida	200			
Indian	95			
low-calorie potato & chives	90			
potato	205			
potato with chives	205			
potato & frankfurter	225			
premium-quality coleslaw	135			
sweetcorn	135			
three-bean	155			
tzatziki	100			
vegetable madras	205			
Waldorf	220			

Food Category or Brand	Calories /100 g	Portion	Size /g	Calories /port
St Michael (Marks & Spencer)				
carrot & nut	253			
cauliflower & apple	224			
Florida	205			
three-bean	148			
Waldorf	301			
Tesco				
brown rice	164	1 pot	250	410
brown rice & vegetables	106	1 pot	250	265
carrot & nut	176	1 pot	250	440
celery, nut & sultana	216	1 pot	250	540
three-bean	144	1 pot	250	360
vegetable	183	1 pot	227	415
Waldorf	165	1 pot	200	330
FRESH				
continental	15	1 packet	200	30
continental mixed	17	1 packet	200	35
country	27	1 packet	200	55
crunchy cauliflower	57	1 packet	200	115
crunchy nut	55	1 packet	200	110
four seasons	17	1 packet	200	35
high-fibre	65	1 packet	200	130
summer	17	1 packet	200	35
Waitrose				
Bombay potato	177			
cabbage & carrot	69			
cabbage & pepper	19			
carnival	129			
carrot, mooli & raisin	71			
celery, nut & sultana	201			
chopped herring	195			
courgette & mushroom	105			

Food Category or Brand	Calories /100 g	Portion	Size /g	Calories /port
five-bean	264			
Indian bean	178			
Italian pasta	150			
Jersey potato	316			
leek & bean	145			
Mexican bean	148			
mixed cabbage	21			
potato & frankfurter	230			
seafood salad	127			
shredded carrot	24			
spicy bean	132			
sprouting bean	137			
tabouleh	97			
tumeric rice	141			
tuna & pasta	136			
Waldorf with fresh mayonnaise	416			
wild rice	195			

Vegetarian Dishes

The dishes included here are manufactured ready-made meals aimed at the 'vegetarian' market. You will also find some vegetarian items in the **Ready-made Meals** section. Some of these dishes would not be suitable for vegans as they contain cow's milk, eggs, etc.

This section includes vegetable-based meat substitutes, such as TVP (textured vegetable protein) and Quorn, which is a myco-protein grown from a tiny fungus. Quorn is low in fat and saturated fat, cholesterol-free and a good source of fibre. A typical serving of Quorn contains 55 calories as against the 300 calories in a portion of roast chicken which included some skin. A portion of soya mince (TVP) is about 80 calories.

Tofu is soya bean curd: the firm type has been pressed and is useful for deep-frying; the most common version is called silken tofu and has the consistency of cream — it is usually made into dips and sauces. Tofu is low in calories and fats.

Vegetarian dishes are often thought of as 'healthy' but that does not always mean 'slimming'. The features to watch for are the sauces and binders used in these recipes. Manufacturers may use fattening binders to hold their 'roasts' and 'burgers' together. Cheese-based sauces (as in cauliflower cheese) are very fattening.

Food Category or Brand	Calories /100 g	Portion	Size /g	Calories /port

Branded Vegetarian Meals

Asda
onion bhaji		each		75
vegetable pakora	321			
vegetable samosa		each		60
vegetable spring rolls		each		165

Batchelors Beanfeasts
American style		1 packet		345
Chinese style		1 packet		240

Bejam / Iceland
cauliflower cheese		1 packet		355
cheese & onion crisp		each		230
vegetable burger		each		165
vegetable grills		each		160
vegetable & nut cutlet		each		165
vegetable sausage		each		130
vegetables au gratin		1 packet		285
vegetable waffles		each		110

Be Well
AMAZING GRAINS
cereal savour	296			
mixed grain vegetable paella	329			
savoury couscous	293			
sultan's pilaff	350			

EASY BEANS
bean stew mix		1 packet	155	505
haricot bean goulash		1 packet	155	515
lentil curry mix		1 packet	155	520
spaghetti bean bolognese		1 packet	155	500

Food Category or Brand	Calories /100 g	Portion	Size /g	Calories /port
Birds Eye				
cauliflower cheese		1 packet		395
cauliflower cheese quarterpounder		each		220
crispy vegetable finger		each		45
macaroni cheese		1 packet		470
mushroom feast		each		100
mushroom & pasta italie		1 packet		303
original vegetable grill		each		130
original vegetable quarterpounder		each		190
sweet & sour vegetables with rice		1 packet		285
vegetable burger		each		80
vegetable chilli with Mexican rice		1 packet		340
vegetable curry with pilaff rice		1 packet		400
vegetable grill		each		145
vegetable lasagne		1 packet		280
Boots				
country casserole		each		305
lasagne verdi		each		255
mushroom pasta carbonara		each		385
vegetarian curry		each		240
vegetarian goulash		each		240
Cauldron Foods				
country tofuloni	190	1 packet	100	190
mushroom or vegetable pâté	160	1 packet	100	160
original tofu	93			
smoked tofu	118			
spicy tofuloni	210	1 packet	100	210
tofu burgers, all flavours		each		150
tomato & red pepper pâté	165	1 packet	100	165
CRISPY TOFU GRILLS				
farmhouse style		each		140
Italian style		each		145
tandoori style		each		145

Food Category or Brand	Calories /100 g	Portion	Size /g	Calories /port
Dale Pak				
GRILLED				
cauliflower cheese grill	250	each	100	250
cheese & onion crispbake	257	each	113	290
cheese & vegetable burger	294	each	85	250
crumbled vegetable grill	255	each	100	255
golden vegetable crunchie		each		50
macaroni cheese grill	315	each	100	315
quorn & vegetable crispbake	224	each	85	190
ratatouille grill	240	each	100	240
vegetable burger	199	each	78	155
vegetable grill	182	each	85	155
vegetable grill, curry	182	each	85	155
vegetable salad grill	265	each	100	265
vegetable waffle	192	each	65	125
Findus				
broccoli, cheese sauce		1 packet	225	300
cauliflower, cheese sauce		1 packet	225	290
French mushroom flan	224			
French onion flan	231			
green bean & mushroom bake		1 packet	225	270
zucchini lasagne	82			
Froqual				
broccoli & almond soufflé		1 packet	160	255
spinach soufflé		1 packet	160	255
Goodlife				
bean bites	474	1 packet	250	1185
falafel	110	1 packet	200	220
herb bean bangers	98	1 packet	225	220
Mexican cutlets	100	1 packet	175	175
nut cutlets	146	1 packet	175	255
tandoori cutlets	97	1 packet	175	170
vegetable koftas	290	1 packet	250	725

Food Category or Brand	Calories /100 g	Portion	Size /g	Calories /port
vegetable & sesame cutlets	131	1 packet	175	230

Granose
CANNED

beans & mushroom stew	79	1 can	420	330
bologna	167	1 can	284	475
Chinese tofu	60	1 can	420	250
dinner balls	145	1 can	400	580
goulash	54	1 can	425	230
lentil & vegetable casserole	100	1 can	425	425
Mexican bean stew	131	1 can	425	555
mock duck	194	1 can	284	550
nutbrawn	211	1 can	284	600
nut loaf	176	1 can	284	500
nuttolene	298	1 can	284	845
sausalatas	137	1 can	284	390
saviand	199	1 can	284	565
savoury cuts	88	1 can	425	375
savoury pudding	207	1 can	454	940
Soyapro, beef flavour	210	1 can	385	810
Soyapro, chicken flavour	210	1 can	400	840
tender bits	79	1 can	425	335
vegecuts	88	1 can	425	375
vege links	167	1 can	284	475
wieners	210	1 can	385	810

DRY PRODUCTS

burger mix	461			
rissolnut	382			
sausfry	482			

FROZEN

celery burgers	153	1 packet	300	460
lentil dish	114	1 packet	350	400
moussaka	91	1 packet	350	320
muesli fritters	146	1 packet	240	350

Food Category or Brand	Calories /100 g	Portion	Size /g	Calories /port
nut & sesame burgers	328	1 packet	300	985
Oriental casserole	89	1 packet	350	310
savoury roll with tofu	164	1 packet	250	410
soya frankies	317	1 packet	300	950
soya & mushroom burgers	251	1 packet	225	565
vegetable 'n' cheeseburger		1 burger		270
vegetables au gratin	100	1 packet	350	350
vegetarian sausage		1 sausage		90
ROASTS				
lentil	335	1 packet	200	670
Mexican corn	440	1 packet	200	880
nut	488	1 packet	300	1465
sunflower & sesame	488	1 packet	200	975
Hera				
chilli	310	1 packet	200	620
vegetable bolognese	305	1 packet	200	610
vegetable casserole	310	1 packet	200	620
vegetable cottage pie	349	1 packet	215	750
vegetable curry	313	1 packet	200	625
vegetable goulash	313	1 packet	200	625
vegetable stew, with dumplings	323	1 packet	200	645
vegetable stroganoff	380	1 packet	200	760
vegetable supreme	389	1 packet	149	580
Holland & Barrett				
mild vegetable curry	84	1 can	425	355
mixed bean salad	67	1 can	425	285
onion bhaji		each		230
vegetable spring roll		each		310
vindaloo hot vegetable curry	84	1 can	425	355
Itona				
TVP beef chunks	248	1 packet	113	280
TVP minced beef	248	1 packet	113	280

Food Category or Brand	Calories /100 g	Portion	Size /g	Calories /port
Kraft				
cheese & onion pasties	306	each		306
Kikkoman				
firm tofu	71	1 packet	297	210
soft tofu	56	1 packet	297	165
Linda McCartney				
beefless burger		each		190
golden nugget		each		70
Italian topper		each		330
lasagne		each		445
ploughman's pasty		each		410
ploughman's pie		each		360
Prewetts				
bolognese sauce	43	1 packet	400	170
cannelloni	106	1 packet	400	425
lentil stew	69	1 packet	400	275
vegetable casserole	98	1 packet	300	295
vegetable chilli	73	1 packet	300	220
vegetable goulash	53	1 packet	400	210
vegetable lasagne	98	1 packet	300	295
vegetable ravioli	90	1 packet	300	270
Realeat				
FROZEN				
vegeburger		each		150
vege cheeseburger		each		155
vegegrill		each		145
vege quarterpounder		each		210
vege quarterpounder with cheese		each		310
Response				
chilli vegetariani	69	1 packet	325	225
leek & pecan pancakes	92	1 packet	325	300
red dragon pie	79	1 packet	340	270
spicy garbanzo beans	65	1 packet	325	210

Food Category or Brand	Calories /100 g	Portion	Size /g	Calories /port
Safeway				
onion bhaji	187			
potato, cheese & onion pasty	291			
vegetable samosa	240			
vegetable savoury bake		each		140
vegetable spring roll	178			
QUORN READY MEALS				
ratatouille	105	pack	340	357
Bombay masala	96	pack	340	326
vegetable spring roll	244	each	175	427
Sainsbury's				
cauliflower cheese flan	240	½ flan		455
cheese & onion flan	275	½ flan		460
chick pea dahl	90	1 can	400	360
fresh vegetable pasty		each		340
hot madras vegetable curry	95	1 can	400	380
Indian delhi vegetable curry	95	1 can	400	380
mushroom quiche	250	½ flan		460
potato, cheese & onion pasty		each		390
vegetable burger		each		105
vegetable grills		each		190
vegetable pie		1 serving		300
vegetable rolls	310	each		35
St Michael (Marks & Spencer)				
broccoli quiche	234			
cauliflower cheese crisp	146	1 packet	113	165
cheese crispbake	235	1 packet	113	265
cheese & onion quiche	300			
cheese pancake	221			
cheese & tomato quiche	280			
leek & mushroom crispbake	173	1 packet	113	195
lemon dahl	143	1 packet	200	285
mushroom curry	107		28	30

Food Category or Brand	Calories /100 g	Portion	Size /g	Calories /port
mushroom quiche	254			
onion bhajis		each		70
vegetable crispbake	133	1 packet	113	150
vegetable cutlet with nuts		each		205
vegetable cutlets	128	1 packet	227	290
vegetable flan	228			
vegetable loaf in tomato sauce	95	1 packet	550	525
vegetable & nut roll	155	1 packet	362	560
vegetable samosas	339		28	95
Sharwood's				
channa dahl	140	1 can	425	595
chick pea dahl	139	1 can	425	590
mild vegetable curry	65	1 can	405	265
onion bhaji mix	331	1 packet	80	265
potato & pea curry	106	1 can	415	440
Waitrose				
aubergine gratin	185			
broccoli & Swiss cheese quiche	200			
cauliflower cheese	76			
nut roast	325		28	91
nut roast with tomato	261		28	73
potato cheese and asparagus pancake	156			
potato dauphinoise	144			
vegetable pulao	135			
vegetable samosa		each		125
Weight Watchers from Heinz				
quorn sweet & sour with rice	286			
Wholefare				
vegetable & seed crumble	117	1 packet	300	350

Index of Foods

Some foods may appear in more than one place. The page numbers refer to the beginning of the relevant sections.

Of further interest . . .

THE FOOD COMBINING DIET

Lose weight the Hay way

Kathryn Marsden

NO COUNTING CALORIES
NO SMALL PORTIONS
FEW FORBIDDEN FOODS

Leading nutritionist Kathryn Marsden has devised four weeks of easy recipes which include three meals a day, already divided into the three food categories of STARCH, PROTEIN, and ALKALINE meals.

The recipes can either be followed strictly day by day or mixed and matched by more confident food combiners.

There are useful health tips and simple explanations as well as ideas for menu planning.

This is not a 'quick fix' diet. Based on the Hay system of Food Combining, this carefully devised eating plan allows you to enjoy your food while you lose weight — safely.

Nothing could be simpler. *The Food Combining Diet* is the perfect introduction to a new way of eating for life.

'Explains so simply how to adopt food combining. Tremendous.' Katie Boyle

'An easy to follow and powerful book.' Leslie Kenton

FOOD COMBINING IN 30 DAYS

The one month health plan that really works

Kathryn Marsden

Following the phenomenal success of *The Food Combining Diet*, Kathryn Marsden has created her 30 DAY DIET PLAN. The brand new approach with a health promise attached.

Everyone is talking about food combining — also known as the Hay diet. Easy to follow, taking one day at a time, this book explains clearly how food combining works — for weight loss, and improving health and vitality. It includes:

- a step by step approach to the food combining rules
- easy recipe ideas divided into starch, protein and alkaline meals
- revitalizing exercises
- Kathryn Marsden's health tips for an improved lifestyle.

After the first week you'll be feeling better than ever before. By the end of day 30 you'll be feeling fit for life.

SLIM THE VEGETARIAN WAY

The healthy way to lose weight

Leah Leneman

Nothing could be simpler than slimming the vegetarian way.

Here are 52 menus, one for every week of the year — making the most of seasonal fruits and vegetables and including pasta, pulses and nutty dishes too.

Leah Leneman concentrates on what you *can* eat instead of what you should avoid. Every meal is calorie counted and allows for plenty of variety. There are ideas for occasional desserts too.

By following the guidelines you can be confident that you will be getting all the nutrients you need, without putting on weight.

Whether or not you are vegetarian you will enjoy the recipes in this book.

IT'S THE POSITIVELY HEALTHY WAY TO LOSE WEIGHT.

THE JUICING DETOX DIET

The new way to total health

Caroline Wheater

Juicing! It's the simple way to revitalize your life – boost your vitamin and mineral levels – and give yourself a kick start on the road to optimum health.

Healthy, easy to prepare and delicious tasting, fruit and vegetable juices are packed with goodness and are the perfect addition to our fast, modern lifestyles.

So – juice it up – starting with an easy detox diet. Choose your favourite fruits and vegetables and try out:

THE ONE DAY JUICE PLAN
THE WEEKEND CLEAN-UP PLAN
THE ONE WEEK AND TWO WEEK VITALITY PLANS

Here is everything you need to know about preparing, mixing and using juices. Plus tips on how to pamper yourself while following your juicing plan.

It's *the* keep fit program – for *inner* health and beauty.

ALSO FROM CAROLINE WHEATER: *JUICING FOR HEALTH*.

E FOR ADDITIVES

The best-selling, award-winning definitive E number guide

**Maurice Hanssen
with Jill Hanssen**

This book cracks the 'E' number code and enables you to understand the lists of additives that appear on the packs of the food you buy, so that you can see exactly what has been added, where it comes from, why it has been added, what it does to the food and — if anything — what it might do to you.

Here is all you need to know about:

- Which additives are natural and which can have harmful effects
- The reasons behind the use of preservatives, colours and flavourings in our foods
- How to make informed choices when you shop
- Additives in wine and vitamin supplements
- Additives in meat
- Guidelines on acceptable daily intake

This vital guide has led a consumer revolution, causing the food industry to re-think its policy on additives. No one who is concerned with the quality of the food they eat can afford to be without this invaluable reference book.

Maurice Hanssen wins Glenfiddich Special Award for excellence in food and wine writing — E for Additives "... has done more than any other publication to persuade the food industry that unnecessary over-processing is not in their interest or the interest of the public." — Derek Cooper, award judge, in *The Listener*.

THE FOOD COMBINING DIET	0 7225 2790 X	£4.99	☐
FOOD COMBINING IN 30 DAYS	0 7225 2960 0	£4.99	☐
FOOD COMBINING FOR HEALTH	0 7225 2506 0	£4.99	☐
FOOD COMBINING FOR VEGETARIANS	0 7225 2763 2	£4.99	☐
SLIM THE VEGETARIAN WAY	0 7225 2807 8	£3.99	☐
THE JUICING DETOX DIET	0 7225 2838 8	£3.99	☐
JUICING FOR HEALTH	0 7225 2839 6	£4.99	☐
E FOR ADDITIVES	0 7225 1562 6	£5.99	☐

All these books are available from your local bookseller or can be ordered direct from the publishers.

To order direct just tick the titles you want and fill in the form below:

Name: _____

Address: _____

_____

_____ Postcode: _____

Send to: Thorsons Mail Order, Dept 3, HarperCollins*Publishers*, Westerhill Road, Bishopbriggs, Glasgow G64 2QT.
Please enclose a cheque or postal order or your authority to debit your Visa/Access account —

Credit card no: _____

Expiry date: _____

Signature: _____

— to the value of the cover price plus:
UK & BFPO: Add £1.00 for the first book and 25p for each additional book ordered.
Overseas orders including Eire: Please add £2.95 service charge. Books will be sent by surface mail but quotes for airmail despatches will be given on request.

24 HOUR TELEPHONE ORDERING SERVICE FOR ACCESS/VISA CARDHOLDERS — TEL: 041 772 2281.